F. Matthias Alexander
The Man and his Work

Lulie Westfeldt was born in New Orleans in 1895. She was a magna cum laude graduate of Sophie Newcomb College where she majored in English. She worked as a social worker at Kinglsey House, a settlement house, in New Orleans, after which she moved to New York. She travelled often, especially in the Northeast U.S. and in England.

Lulie Westfeldt had poliomyelitis as a child and underwent several orthopedic operations which aggravated her difficulties. In 1929 she had a series of lessons with F. M. Alexander and decided soon afterwards to train, joining Alexander's first training course in 1931.

Upon completion of the teacher training course in 1934 she started teaching in North America. In 1937 she moved to New York where for many years she was the only teacher of the Alexander Technique. In 1950 she bought a country residence at Sandgate, Vermont, where she also taught the Technique. She was a devout Episcopalian and her interests included painting and horse-riding.

Her book, *F. M. Alexander: The Man and his Work*, was first published in 1964. Lulie Westfeldt died in 1965.

Lulie Westfeldt in 1962

Lulie Westfeldt

F. Matthias Alexander:
The Man and His Work

Memoirs of training in the Alexander Technique 1931–34

Mouritz

First published 1964 simultaneously by
Associated Booksellers, Westport, Connecticut
and by Allen & Unwin, London
Paperback facsimile edition October 1986
by Centerline Press, California

Second edition published February 1998 by
Mouritz
6 Ravenslea Road
London SW12 8SB
United Kingdom

© 1998 The Estate of Lulie Westfeldt

ISBN 0–9525574–2–8 Paperback

A CIP Catalogue record for this book
is available from the British Library

Cover design, layout and
typesetting by Jean M. O. Fischer
Printed on 90 gsm High Opaque
and bound in Great Britain by
Redwood Books, Trowbridge, Wiltshire

Cover photograph of F. M. Alexander
in 1941, courtesy of © Walter Carrington

This book is dedicated to
CATHERINE WIELOPOLSKA
with love and gratitude

Contents

List of illustrations	IX
Author's note and acknowledgements	XI
Author's preface	XII
John Dewey on F. M. Alexander	XVI

Part One
Training with F. M. Alexander 1931-1934

1. My introduction to Alexander's work	3
2. My first series of lessons	18
3. Early days of the training course	32
4. Gradual change in my outlook on Alexander	43
5. Our progress in learning—some of the changes the work brought about in pupils	57
6. Alexander and opportunities	65
7. *The Merchant of Venice*	71
8. Learning to be teachers	81
9. A personal experience	86
10. Postscript to the teacher's training course	93
11. My teaching experience in New York City	99

Part Two
Alexander's discoveries

12. Alexander's discovery of the HN & B pattern	125
13. Detailed discussion of the head, neck and back relationship	134
14. Other discoveries of Alexander's	146
15. Alexander's technique of inhibition	152
16. Summary and evaluation	157

PART THREE
APPENDIXES

A. Clarification of terms 1) and 2)   163
B. Comments of John Dewey, Sir Charles Sherrington and G. E. Coghill on Alexander's search and discovery   164
C. Review by Marjory Barlow of Lulie Westfeldt's *F. Matthias Alexander*   168
D. Two letters on *Hamlet*   171
E. Newspaper reviews of *Hamlet*   172

Index   174

ILLUSTRATIONS

Frontispiece Lulie Westfeldt (Courtesy of Alice Westfeldt Mathews)
John Dewey and F. M. Alexander (Courtesy of Walter Carrington), p. XVI.

Fig. 1   F. M. Alexander in 1941 (Courtesy of S.T.A.T.), p. 20.
Fig. 2   Members of the first training course in 1931 (Courtesy of Erika Whitaker), p. 33.
Fig. 3   F. M. Alexander on holiday, Summer 1939, at 'Exe', The Hard, Bognor Regis, Sussex (Courtesy of Brian Campbell), p. 38.
Fig. 4   On the Verandah at Penhill, *c.* 1931 (Courtesy of Walter Carrington), p. 40.
Fig. 5   F. M. Alexander and his wife, Edith Mary (Courtesy of S.T.A.T.), p. 47.
Fig. 6   Passport photographs of Lulie Westfeldt in 1929 and 1933, p. 60.
Fig. 7   Nike (Winged Victory) of Samothrace, (Courtesy of Kunstakademiets Bibliotek, Copenhagen), p. 63
Fig. 8   Programme for *The Merchant of Venice*, page 1 and 2 (Courtesy of Walter Carrington), p. 72.
Fig. 9   Programme for *Hamlet*, page 1 and 3 (Courtesy of Walter Carrington), p. 74.
Fig. 10 Programme for Hamlet, page 2 (Courtesy of Walter Carrington), p. 75.
Fig. 11 Charles Neil, Gurney MacInnes and Irene Stewart in *Hamlet*, 1934 (Courtesy of Walter Carrington), p. 78.
Fig. 12 Gurney MacInnes and George Trevelyan in *Hamlet*, 1934 (Courtesy of Walter Carrington), p. 78
Fig. 13 Students in *Hamlet*, 1934 (Courtesy of Walter Carrington), p. 79.
Fig. 14 Lulie in 1952 (Courtesy of Alice Westfeldt Mathews), p. 90.
Fig. 15 Nora's cat drawing, p. 106.

Fig. 16   Egyptian statue illustrating the integration of the pelvis with the back, *c.* 1950 BC. (Courtesy of the Metropolitan Museum of Art, Gift of Jules S. Backe, 1925. (25.6)), p. 136.
Fig. 17   Head forward and up, p. 138.
Fig. 18   Head too far forward, p. 139.
Fig. 19   German suit of armour showing how the arms are placed when the HN & B pattern is working, *c.* 1549 (Courtesy of the Metropolitan Museum of Art, Rogers Fund and Pratt Gift, 1933. (33.164a-x)), p. 140.
Fig. 20   Italian suit of armour showing the extraordinary grace in walking if the HN & B pattern is working, *c.* 1480 (Courtesy of the Metropolitan Museum of Art, Bashford Dean Memorial Collection, Gift of Edward S. Harkness, 1929 (29.156.66)), p. 141.
Fig. 21   Statue of Etruscan warrior showing the kind of knee-thrust a man has if the HN & B pattern is working, 20th century AD in style of 5th century BC (Courtesy of the Metropolitan Museum of Art, Purchase, 1921 (21.195)), p. 143.
Fig. 22   A Greek statuette which shows some of the deformities the body can get into when the HN & B pattern is not working, Hellenistic Period (Courtesy of the Metropolitan Museum of Art, Fletcher Fund, 1924 (24.73)), p. 145.
Fig. 23   Eight-month old baby, sitting attained without adult aid, and sitting as pulled to sitting position by adult. From Alma Frank's 'A Study in Infant Development' in *Child Development* Vol. 9, no. 1, March 1938 (The Society for Research in Child Development, National Research Council, Washington, D. C.), p. 151.

Author's Note

The head, neck and back pattern discovered and made active by Alexander, in himself and others, has, at all times, existed in human beings. Often we see its manifestations represented in art—be it stylized art or representational art.

In the Winged Victory (Nike) of Samothrace, page 63, for example, we can all see the upward flow of energy within the human figure to a marked degree.

I am including a few pictures that illustrate certain manifestations of the pattern which we will discuss in the book.

Acknowledgments

I wish to acknowledge and thank the friends and pupils who have helped me so generously in the many problems that have occurred in the writing and the launching of this book: Jim Becket, Jane Lillibridge, Mrs John Knox Jessup, Jr., Rick Williams, Dr and Mrs Clark Foreman, Dr and Mrs Donald Mainland, Dr Millard Smith, Mr and Mrs Robertson Davies, John Black, Dr David Wolfe, Mrs Leconte Du Nouy, Mrs Alfred Wielopolska and Mrs Lawrence Saunders.

Lulie Westfeldt

Publisher's Note

The publishers would like to acknowledge Mrs Marjory Barlow for permission to include her review (appendix C).

Figures 1, 2, 4, 5, 7–14 and 23, the frontispiece, the photograph on page XVI and the appendixes C, D and E are all new to this edition.

Author's Preface

In the summer of 1904 there appeared upon the London scene a young Australian named Frederick Matthias Alexander, the originator of a unique system of physical and mental re-education which he called the Alexander Technique and which is the subject of this book.

Alexander visited the United States twice and was sponsored by such men as James Harvey Robinson, John Dewey, who wrote introductions to three of his books, and the biologist G. E. Coghill, who wrote a foreword to his fourth and last book. It was in England, however, where he lived, that Alexander's work achieved wide recognition, as is attested by his obituary notice in the London *Times* of October 11, 1955. I quote it in full:

> Mr F. M. Alexander, 'F.M.' as he liked to be called, died at his home in London yesterday at the age of 86. An Australian, he was born in 1869 and after some experience in secretarial posts in Tasmania and Melbourne, set up as a professional reciter. He developed some difficulty in voice production early in his chosen career which orthodox treatment failed to cure. After long experiment he evolved a system of muscular control which he found had very much wider application in the age-old controversial field of mind and body. His technique, which he first taught in Melbourne and then in Sydney, attracted wide attention and he came to London in 1904 to seek an even wider field for his endeavours. In this he was not disappointed, for one of the first to consult him was Sir Henry Irving. Thereafter he had a great connection with the stage and this, as time passed, was extended to many other spheres. Among those who consulted him were Viola Tree, Constance Collier, Lily Brayton, Oscar Asche, Matheson Lang, Bernard Shaw, Aldous Huxley, the late Lord Lytton, Archbishop William Temple and Sir Stafford and Lady Cripps. Among his published works were *Man's Supreme Inheritance* and *Constructive Conscious Control of the Individual*.

Author's Preface XIII

As a student and teacher of his methods, I should like to emphasize at the outset that the 'system of muscular control' mentioned in *The Times* notice is based upon a discovery of revolutionary significance that Alexander made in his study of the human organism. After nine years of experimentation upon himself and others, he found that a certain dynamic relationship of the head, neck and back can be brought into operation; and that this relationship, or pattern, integrates all bodily movement, bringing about the best use of the whole organism as well as of each specific part. In a very few human beings this relationship works perfectly; in many more it works imperfectly, and in the greatest number it can hardly be said to work in anything but a vestigial fashion.

The relationship exists potentially in every human body except in cases of extreme pathology or where certain forms of drastic surgery have been used. Even in individuals where it has been damaged by disease, surgery or malformation it can be re-awakened and put to work when it has fallen into disuse. Because of the intimate association between use and functioning, such restoration is followed by improvement both physical and mental,* sometimes to an amazing degree and in realms where it might not be expected to penetrate.

Alexander called the pattern he discovered the Primary Control. The term is not a happy one as it is ambiguous and lends itself to misunderstanding. In this book it will be called the *HN & B* pattern, the letters HN & B standing, of course, for the words 'head, neck and back.'

One of my most difficult tasks in the pages which follow is to explain the importance of Alexander's discovery without seeming to make absurd claims for it. For those who are unfamiliar with his work and think that I have overstated its results, I can say that I, personally, have benefited from it far more than I expected or hoped.

It is true that I had not hoped for much. At the age of seven I had had poliomyelitis and I went to Alexander when I was 34 years old. Behind me lay disheartening years of surgery and other orthodox therapies that had not only failed to

---

* See Appendix A, Clarification of Terms, p. 163.

improve my condition but had left me with added physical handicaps and disastrous psychological scars. The practical application of Alexander's technique re-made my life and I have seen it benefit and often re-make the lives of hundreds of other people suffering from a great variety of functional disorders.

But my harshest critics are likely to be those who are familiar with Alexander's work and, having seen its results for themselves, will charge me with calculated understatement. To these I can only say that I prefer it so.

The reader will probably wonder a little how Alexander's discovery applies to him. The words used in describing it may call up to his mind a rather dull limited region, and it may be hard for him to see how anything like this could give help and power in meeting ordinary day-to-day problems. Let him but ask the men and women who have experienced Alexander's work, and they will tell him that there is no problem in an individual's life to which this work is not applied. It is used by the businessman in an interview, the actor at an audition, the woman in childbirth, the housewife in her work, the pianist at a concert, the singer, the dancer, the golfer, the rider; it is used by a wide variety of people in all situations that require their highest skill and competence. It is used by the shy, the awkward, and above all, the tired.

The work of a man cannot, in most instances, be separated from the man himself, and a picture of Alexander, describing his eccentricities and limitations, as well as his very great gifts, should be of service to the understanding of his work. Always I meet two opposing attitudes about Alexander. The first regards him as an archetypal hero; this results in the cult and worship of his personality without judgement or discrimination. The second one regards him as partly a charlatan but a charlatan who in some inexplicable way seems to have done great things for many people.

But with those who worship and those who criticize, as well as those who have heard his name for the first time, there is always puzzlement. Undoubtedly an aura of great achievement hangs about his name. Why then, people wonder, is his work not better known and more established in the world today? How can it be that his discovery, which has given new life to people numbering in the thousands, is an *unknown factor* in the therapies of today? This is what the public cannot understand, and so with the half-knowledge that they have they lose interest in the man and too easily dismiss his work.

It is the aim of this book to clear up this confusion, to complete this knowledge, and cause the pieces of this puzzle to fall into place. It will then be recognized that the surprising thing is not that this work is not more widely established but that it is alive at all and that its very survival in the face of so many difficulties bespeaks its worth.

I was a member of Alexander's first training course for teachers and was in close contact with him for a period of ten years. For four years I had daily contact except for two or three months during the year. I have taught his technique for twenty-six years. This is the background upon which I base my discussion of the man and his work.

There are various types of writing in this book. In Part One there is narrative, case history, and exposition. At first glance it might be supposed that the narration would have the greatest appeal. In point of fact, however, it is the exposition, the story of Alexander's discoveries in Part Two, that has had the greatest hold on the few persons who have seen it so far. As one reader remarked, 'It holds one as an adventure story holds one, this tale of a solitary man's discovery in the face of overwhelming difficulties.'

Lulie Westfeldt

John Dewey
on the work of F. M. Alexander

John Dewey wrote introductions to three of F. M. Alexander's books. These quotations are from two of them.

> It bears the same relation to education that education itself bears to life.
>
> <div align="right">Introduction to <i>The Use of the Self</i></div>

> It contains in my jugdement the promise and potentiality of the new direction that is needed in all education.
>
> Ibid.

> Personally, I cannot speak with too much admiration—in the original sense of wonder as well as the sense of respect—of the persistence and thoroughness with which these extremely difficult observations and experiments were carried out.
>
> Ibid.

> Mr Alexander has demonstrated a new scientific principle with respect to the control of human behaviour, as important as any principle which has ever been discovered in the domain of external nature.
>
> <div align="right">Introduction to <i>Constructive Conscious Control of the Individual</i></div>

PART ONE

TRAINING WITH F. M. ALEXANDER

1931-1934

Chapter 1

My introduction to Alexander's work

On a day in the early spring of 1929, I went to the old L. & N. railway station in New Orleans, which was my home, to meet one of my best friends from the north. She was coming to pay me a long-anticipated visit.

It was an exciting moment to see her happy, vital face coming through the gloom of the station, and after we had exchanged our greetings and most important bits of news, we hurried to the baggage room to pick up her suitcase. In the flurry of reunion we forgot something, a book. Returning to the baggage room, there it was lying on an old crate—a book with a title that seemed rather vague: *Man's Supreme Inheritance*, by a man I had never heard of—F. Matthias Alexander.

So it happened that I first met, by the sight of his name on a book, a man with whom I was to have a close personal and professional association for many years and whose work was to influence my life and thought from that day on.

It seemed to me that my friend Catherine attached an immoderate importance to this book. 'What is it about?' I asked her, as I turned the Ford off Canal Street on our way home.

'Muscular co-ordination,' said Catherine, 'but lots of other things as well.'

Instantly I had a feeling of dismay. I had so looked forward to her coming—it was always such fun discussing things with her—but now, were we going to have to discuss this? And my dismay deepened.

The words 'muscular co-ordination' were trigger words for me. I was 31 years old at that time. As a child of seven I had had poliomyelitis. The subsequent history of the therapies that had been tried and their results had created in my mind a block against discussing or even thinking about the body* and how it functioned. To get along one had to obliterate

---

* See Appendix A, Clarification of Terms 1, p. 163.

thinking about such subjects, as much as one could.

It had all started with my first operation, when my right ankle was fixed and rendered immobile. Something was done on the left foot too, but as far as I could see that operation affected neither my gait nor my comfort. It was the ankylosis of the right ankle that started off bad things. Before that operation, I had no conscious difficulty in movement; I could go up and down stairs with ease, I could run, I could climb hills. I did not know exactly what my gait looked like. I had a dropped foot, but as long as I could do what I wanted to do, I paid no attention to it except when I saw the effect it had on other people and other children; then I was disturbed and sometimes frightened. The adults were apt to convey pity through their faces or their voices; the children were curious and prying or sometimes cruel. It was, however, the attitude of others and not any crushing physical difficulty or discomfort that was my handicap at that time. I could wear low shoes, I could go barefoot. There were no special dressmaking difficulties—I often had ready-made clothes and these required no special alteration beyond shortening.

It was six years between the time I had polio in 1903 and that first operation fixing the right ankle. Some of my back muscles had been affected by polio, and yet in those six years there was only a very faint divergence from the normal in my appearance; what the mirror showed was hardly noticeable. The family snapshots showed up nothing. In the summers I went to my grandfather's farm in western North Carolina; it was almost a family settlement, as the various sons and daughters came with their children and innumerable snapshots were taken and pasted in albums. Each summer was recorded in these albums. There is nothing distinguishing me from anyone else in these albums prior to this first operation, but after that operation there was a marked difference. Perhaps I have given too rosy a picture of my state. My gait must have been bad, as it impressed others that way, I tired more easily, had less speed in running, was less secure on a horse, but nevertheless I rarely, if ever, felt myself impeded in doing the things I wanted to do. My real affliction was the community outlook on my gait.

When the doctor who performed the operation on my ankle was examining me once he said, 'We'll have you running like any other little girl.' I was too shy to say, 'I can run now.'

For years afterwards I remembered those words of his, and I would think in a puzzled way, 'Doesn't a doctor really know that a fixed ankle forever does away with running?'

After the ankle operation when I was 13 things went wrong rapidly. The operation was in February 1909; around April or May I heard one member of my family say to another (not knowing that I heard), 'She is getting very crooked since that operation.' Walking was vastly more difficult, but I at first did not yet look on this as a permanent thing. I thought it was simply weakness from not using my feet and legs after the operation, and I assumed that it would disappear in time. When I got off crutches, I kept the crutches in a closet and when I was by myself, I would use them again, it was so much easier and more comfortable. No one liked to see me use them, so I did it only when by myself. I could no longer go upstairs with my right foot, but here again I thought this was mere weakness that would in time disappear.

In the summer holidays at my grandfather's farm there were hills and mountains everywhere. I found to my dismay that I now had the greatest difficulty in climbing these hills. Between my father's white cottage and my grandfather's big stone house a steep hill rose sharply from a mountain spring. We children used to love to run up and down this hill. We had favourite trees along the way; they were rather special to us; and we used to tell them goodbye when we left in the fall for the long winter in school. Now I found that I could not get up this hill at all except by walking backwards and forwards in long zigzag paths which lessened the slope. Rather than do this, it was easier to go by the carriage road which was a roundabout way and much longer. It commenced to dawn on me that my difficulty in climbing hills and going up stairs, my inability to run or even walk fast, was not because my muscles were weak, but because my ankle was no longer a joint.

I remember in detail my surroundings when this full realization came to me. I was in a honeysuckle thicket near our cottage. I remember the sight and smell of the honeysuckle in bloom and the sound of a nearby stream. My sister and I had made tunnels in it, and I was sitting in one of these tunnels thinking I would go back to the house. There was a moderate-size hill separating me from the house, and I began to figure out what would be the best way for me to get up it. Full awareness came to me then for a moment: 'It is not because of weak muscles that will finally get strong that walking is so difficult—it is because you have no ankle joint.' I thought, 'You will never be able to get up hills or climb stairs as you used to do—you will never be able to run or even walk fast—this is going to last all of your life.' The minute that awareness came, I shut it off as if I had closed a door. Thoughts like that must never be allowed to come up, and if they did, they must be blotted out at once.

Thus I got farther and farther away from the actual situation. A fear, which was kept below the surface, grew, and a sense of fate came into being and also grew! I was always going to have bad luck; things were never going to work out well for me. It was not simply my physical devastation that had upset my world—*they* had been wrong. Doctors and well-meaning relatives, those you looked to for guidance and help, they had said I would be greatly improved by these operations. Now they were silent. Whom could one turn to? There was no one to turn to, there was just fate, and I was afraid of fate.

Additional physical difficulties came and fed this outlook. Gradually my right heel drew up and was no longer able to touch the ground. I was more comfortable standing in a heel moderately high, and yet in walking I had no balance or security in such a heel. It was a vicious circle. It was impossible now for me to go barefoot or to wear a sandal. I could not with any comfort or balance wear low shoes or slippers. I had slippers to wear to parties; but a great deal of shopping about had to be done to find a pair that would be possible for me to walk in, and even then I would be conscious of every step and mindful of my balance.

In ordinary everyday life, high shoes were a necessity for me. This meant I could rarely be satisfied about how I looked in my clothes. Only heavy tailor-made clothes looked in any way suitable with high shoes, and those I wore—hot climate or no hot climate. There was a short vogue at that time of wearing spats, only the vogue was not short for me! With spats on, one might be supposed to have on low shoes underneath. I wore spats so long after everyone else had forgotten about them that ordinary high shoes would have attracted much less attention.

Still another thing that took place was that when I used my right foot my balance was unevenly distributed and all my weight was thrown on one particular spot—a spot slightly back of the little toe. A callous formed, and in spite of help from chiropodists and a pad worn just back of the callous, every step was uncomfortable; and after a number of years every step was painful.

In addition to my shoe difficulties, I was having dressmaking difficulties as well; my body was getting out of kilter rapidly—the back, the shoulders, the hips. It was as if before the operation my body was being thrown slightly out of line by the effects of polio; now this was happening rapidly and markedly.

The process I had started of blocking off anything that pertained to the body went on. I threw myself into school life and its activities and later on into college life and its activities. It was interesting and satisfying and by and large a happy time. My college photographs show me to be an exhausted, strained creature, but I never gave that a second's thought; it didn't interest me.

Life went on more or less in this pattern until I was 27 years old. Several factors converged then to make me seek help again. For one thing, I had some extra money which made it possible for me to consider further help, and I was willing to consider it because my difficulties seemed to be getting too much for me and were forcing themselves upon my notice. It was clear to me that I was getting worse.

I thought things over carefully; maybe it was the operation of fixing a joint that was harmful; other kinds of operations might help. Also I felt that the greatest care must be taken in selecting a doctor; I was helped in this by a woman who worked with polio children throughout a certain state and who had a wide experience with many orthopaedic doctors. I went to the one whom she considered the best in the country for my particular difficulties. He advised realigning the right foot and having a tendon transplantation on the left foot. I had this done.

The realignment of my right foot resulted in some improvement; my weight was better distributed so that when taking a step the callous was uncomfortable rather than painful. At first I thought the gait of my left foot had improved. In slightly over a year, however, a new kind of wrongness set in. My left shoulder hunched up with every movement. A friend later told me she thought I had adopted a sort of collegiate mannerism. I also noticed I was getting increasingly out of kilter and that my left shoulder-blade was protruding markedly. I asked a trained nurse about this once and questioned her as to whether my new shoulder habit and other retrogression could possibly be linked up with transplanting tendons in my left foot. She said yes, this operation was intended to increase mobility, but that it could also increase deformity, in that it was sometimes very hard to execute the job so that the balance would be just right—it could tend in time to pull one askew.

Many years later I asked a young medical interne the same question. He said there were instruments, measuring instruments I believe, used by surgeons which enabled them to get a perfect balance in the transplantation of tendons. I do not know which one was right or whether at the time of my operation the instruments the interne spoke of were in use. Whatever the explanation, my own experience with specific therapies was a harsh one and something I never willingly thought about.

But now on this spring day in 1929 as I talked with Catherine these old scars were again being brought to the surface, so as one sometimes does in a distasteful situation that one cannot get out of, I acted. I was there on the surface but the real me was detached, floating off in space somewhere. I talked a great deal and while this talk was intended to be just a show I was putting on, yet some of it was helpful to me. I explained to Catherine that Alexander and his work could never have any connection with me personally. In the first place I had not money enough to cross the ocean, much less to take lessons which seemed at that time vastly expensive—three to four guineas a lesson (which was the equivalent of $15 to $20). I reassured myself with this talk and built up a sense of safety. I kept on and explained to Catherine that while this new work might have much to offer the ordinary body, it would never be of use to me. Not only had there been actual destruction in my body at the time I had polio but in addition to that there had been surgical interference later on. Thus having settled the matter that the work could have no connection with me, I could almost allow myself to be placidly interested in Alexander's book from a detached intellectual standpoint, and I was anxious to be interested. Catherine was very dear to me and she was fired with enthusiasm about this new idea. I wanted to be able to meet her enthusiasm with friendly interest.

Her outlook was in direct contrast to mine. She had always had an unusually deep interest in health and because of this had trained as a nurse. But her hospital experience had become less and less satisfying to her. She thought that the emphasis was too much on the symptoms of the disease and too little on what led up to the disease and how the general resistance of the body might be strengthened. (This was about 1926.) She said distressingly often a patient would be 'cured' and sent home to return soon with another disease. So she was seeking another field that would offer her a convincing programme of rehabilitation and preventive medicine where she could feel that her work had real importance in contributing to health. She hoped for something that would treat the organism in a less fragmentary way.

It was a few years after her hospital experience that she first heard of Alexander. His work, she said, was based on something he called a Primary Control. He used these words to describe a relationship of the head, neck and back in which the neck became progressively freer, the head tended to go forward in relation to the neck and up, and the back tended to lengthen and widen. When this relationship or pattern is working, all parts of the body involved in use and movement work cooperatively together and to the best advantage. Such right use in the ordinary activities of everyday life had a dramatically powerful effect on functioning, posture, bodily contours, and alignment. Various deformities as well as various forms of malfunctioning cleared up or were improved.

'His work seemed to answer questions that had been lying dormant and unanswered with me for years,' Catherine said. She went on to add that if there were a Primary Control and Alexander could teach one to use it, then she wanted to know all about it firsthand, as it seemed to her to offer a more sound and more powerful way of affecting the general health of the individual than any she had yet heard of.

She said when you looked at a group in any clinic, the first thought that came to mind was, 'How could that patient's heart, kidneys, or liver work properly?' The people she had worked with in clinics were bent over, sway-backed, with loss of height and other deformities. She thought that Alexander's discovery could give at least a part of the answer as to why, when we are given such fine bodies, such dreadful deterioration accumulates in them as life goes on.

Other factors might contribute, of course, and among clinic patients one might at first think of poverty as being an important cause; but then one saw just as many misshapen bodies among those who were not poor.

'I felt that the right use of one's body,' she said, 'was too important a thing to be neglected and that it might well be a basic factor in preventive medicine.'

Catherine's first knowledge of Alexander had not come through a book but through a person, a person who showed in a truly dramatic way the changes that Alexander's work could bring about. Two or three years previously she had seen an old family friend—a Mrs Brown, who was in an alarming state mentally and emotionally, having never recovered from the death of her son. She had a number of physical ailments as well, haemorrhoids, flat feet and constant respiratory trouble, but it was her nervous difficulties that were her greatest trouble.

Encountering Mrs Brown again after several years' interval, Catherine could scarcely believe she was the same person. She no longer had haemorrhoids or difficulty with her feet, and her respiratory troubles were greatly improved. The really startling change, however, was that she was no longer nervously unstrung and depressed; rather she possessed an outlook that was positive, vital and tranquil.

Catherine said to her, 'What on earth has happened to you?' And Mrs Brown replied, 'I have had lessons from F. Matthias Alexander.'

She went on to say how she had read an article by James Harvey Robinson, American historian, in the *Atlantic Monthly* called 'The Philosopher's Stone'; it described the work of F. Matthias Alexander and had so impressed her that she sent out inquiries with a view to locating the man and going to him for lessons.

Robinson's words in dedicating this article to Alexander were: 'These first fruits of a new literature of true freedom are dedicated by the writer to the genius who made the momentous discovery.' For Mrs Brown this article was indeed a 'new literature of true freedom'. Mr Alexander was in the United States in 1919 and she had gone to him in New York. Under his teaching she had been gradually transformed, both as to health and outlook. She told Catherine that it all seemed like a miracle and that after she had worked with him off and on for almost a year she was in command of herself again. It was this contact with Mrs Brown and seeing firsthand this transformation that had occurred in her that first fired Catherine's enthusiasm for Alexander's work. It is doubtful if a book alone could have done this.

We found the book difficult but interesting. In spite of its being excruciatingly badly written (one was continually getting lost in a verbal maze), the originality of the subject-matter stood out and also the compelling conviction on the part of the author that he had made a revolutionary discovery. The book was challenging and the reader wanted to know more. From the book one judged the 'Primary Control' to be the cornerstone of his whole work.

He had discovered this 'Primary Control' in an exhaustive research undertaken to meet an urgent personal need. A reciter and actor by profession, increasing trouble with his voice was jeopardizing his career. Doctors had been unable to help him, though they agreed with his own premise that it was something he was doing with himself when he used his voice that caused his trouble. He set out to discover what this was. The first finding showed him that his voice difficulties were linked up with what he was doing with his head, neck and back. The head, neck and back always functioned together as a pattern. After prolonged experimentation with different patterns of the head, neck and back, he finally discovered one which he called the Primary Control because when he maintained it in speaking and reciting, he completely conquered his voice trouble.

Later on, much to his surprise, he found that in teaching other people how to maintain this pattern he helped them in overcoming a great variety of specific ills to an almost miraculous extent. The 'Primary Control' could be applied not only to voice difficulties but to many other forms of malfunctioning throughout the body. This experience with himself and others was the basis for Alexander's *first* and most important principle which was that a specific defect could best be helped by getting the Primary Control to work rather than using various specific therapies. What he did for a person was always the same, whether he had a pianist who wanted to improve his tone, a man suffering from flat feet, or a woman overridden by nervous tension: he worked to get the new HN & B pattern operating. Certainly his procedure, at any rate, was revolutionary as it ran counter to current medical practice and all other known therapies.

There was also a corollary to this main principle which made a special impact on me. This was that exercises and other specific therapies affecting a specific part could be harmful. To improve one part did not mean that you improved all parts; it most often meant the reverse. He cited a number of convincing instances to illustrate this, and I found the premise itself convincing and reasonable. It had never before entered my head that treating a specific part might in time throw the body as a whole out and that this in turn would in time react adversely on the specific part. Why should this have entered my head? I had never heard of such a thing from a doctor or a layman. You had something the matter with your toe—you had your toe fixed; something the matter with your foot—you had your foot fixed; there was nothing to it. What else could there be to it? I began to consider my right ankle. 'Surely the motion of a joint must be a highly integrated affair,' I thought, 'and if the ankle is fixed and this motion done away with, the whole body will be thrown out. This seems to be what has happened to me.' Once I saw a reason for my deterioration, the superstitious outlook I had acquired began to lose a little of its power. 'Maybe it isn't a sort of doom that has caused me to get worse with every treatment,' I thought, 'maybe it's the treatments themselves.'

My friend's visit ended all too soon and she returned to Philadelphia. She was going to London for thirty lessons with Alexander that summer. I knew she would tell me about her experiences, but I never expected to have a closer connection with the man than that. I did not have sufficient interest to want a closer connection, as I still thought that because of the actual destruction in my body and because of the surgery I had had, Alexander's work would have nothing to offer me. Early that summer things began to happen. A relative died, leaving me a small sum of money. I decided to use this for a trip abroad. I had been once before and thought such travel was more rewarding than anything else one could possibly do. In England I had a stepmother and half-sister; in Paris I had a close friend. The thought of Alexander did not come into my plans. My money was to be spent in having a good time. But once I had written my friend Catherine of my plans, she started her campaign as a high-pressure salesman. She just kept gently and repetitiously at me. It was like the constant notices I had received from a magazine one autumn. For a long time I threw them in the waste-paper basket. Somehow a few seemed to lodge in my desk, and at one point before I knew what had happened I had subscribed to the magazine. My friend's campaign followed the same lines, and I believe something had changed in my outlook before I reached England without my being fully aware of it.

When I arrived in London, Catherine was there with her father in a small hotel off Piccadilly. She was just finishing her course of lessons with Alexander. She had asked me to come to her hotel for a few nights. I remember very vividly going there and ascending in the rickety elevator. Catherine was by the elevator door when I got off, and I was at once struck by her face. It had a new quality. I wondered for a moment what it was and then decided that it was tranquillity. She had always had wonderfully good looks, verve, life, enthusiasm, but not tranquillity. The quality was so new in her that it stood out markedly. As the evening went on, one other change struck me about her: she was no longer a chain smoker. I asked her how she had managed the difficult task of cutting down her smoking. She smiled and said she had done nothing about this herself, but since she had had lessons she no longer had her usual nervous craving for cigarettes. She talked a little about her work with Alexander, but I got no clear impression of how this marked change in her had taken place. She was extremely anxious that I should go and see Alexander with her. I remember she said, 'Take it as a gamble—you don't have to believe it—just take a chance. You have nothing to lose and you might have a lot to gain. Come and see him anyway.'

I was planning to be in London for only a few days at that time as I was going to make some country visits, but I told my friend that when I came back I might go with her to see Alexander.

One of my visits was to my stepmother in Southwold, and when I mentioned to her that I was considering going to see Alexander, she asked me if I would not like to have a letter of introduction to Miss Lucy Silcox, who had been a pupil of Alexander's. Miss Silcox now lived at Boar's Hill, and I was going there to visit my friends the Woods. I said I would be very glad to have such a letter. Miss Silcox had been Headmistress of St Felix's School in Southwold, and her name carried considerable weight in both educational and literary circles.

Soon I went to stay with my old friends Mrs Wood and her daughter Eleanor. I was having an unusually good time. I remember that Eleanor and I drove through some Cotswold villages one afternoon and had a lovely tea somewhere. I squirmed around in the car comfortably and thought, 'Good heavens, maybe in a few weeks I can't be squirming and hunching around in this happy abandoned way. I'll have to think about everything I do.' So, unconsciously, I must have been persuading myself to go to Alexander, and had, without fully knowing it, already crossed the Rubicon. I had told the Woods that I might go to Alexander, and they did not seem to think it was a very sensible idea. They had never heard of Alexander before, and my halting confused presentation of the subject could not have been impressive. When I told Mrs Wood it had to do with ordinary movement such as walking, sitting down, etc., she said, 'Surely there is only one right way to sit down; it can't take long to learn that.'

She was thinking of it more in terms of deportment, I believe, and how, in old-fashioned girls' schools, girls were taught to sit and walk in a way that was considered both ladylike and healthy. Certainly she was not thinking of it in terms of changing one's habitual response to the stimulus of sitting down so that the body as a whole moves in an entirely different pattern.

In the meantime I had sent my letter to Miss Silcox and had received her reply arranging the appointment. Eleanor drove me to her house and left me. Her letter stressed the point that I was to see her alone. I rang the doorbell and a maid opened the door for me and showed me into the drawing-room. It was a lovely room, walls lined with books, soft warm colours about, bowls of flowers, old china—that happy combination of objects and colours so often seen in English drawing-rooms that suggests both culture and cosiness. In a moment Miss Silcox entered the room. She was to me impressive. Her face, because of her eyes and the personality they showed forth, was striking, almost beautiful. Her carriage was erect and graceful, even though she walked with a slight limp.

She told me that she had had a long series of lessons with Alexander. Her trouble, like mine, had started in some form of paralysis. (A fellow teacher and close friend of Miss Silcox's whom I met later believed she had had infantile paralysis, although this was not fully established.)

As she told her story I could see why she had stressed the note of privacy. She would not care to speak to a casual outsider about so deep and personal an experience, though she would be willing to speak to another handicapped person seeking help.

'It was becoming increasingly difficult for me to get out of bed in the morning and dress myself,' she said. Hers was no slight handicap, I thought, and she had the feeling of knowing she was getting worse, too.

Miss Silcox continued. 'At the end of a long period of work with Alexander—I went to him for about a year that first time—I was able to go to Switzerland with a friend on my holidays and do some mountain climbing.'

It took me some time to take this in. Then there seemed only one comment to make. 'Your life was really re-made, Miss Silcox, wasn't it?' I asked.

'Yes,' she said. She told me that her experience with doctors had been similar to mine, that Alexander's system was unique. In her opinion he had added to human knowledge.

Towards the end of our talk, Miss Silcox spoke of how her measurements had changed. I was interested, so she left the room and returned with the measurements her tailor had taken before and after she had had Alexander's work. His last measurements showed that her shoulders had widened, her height increased, and her back had widened! On the other hand, her hips and her waist were considerably smaller than in his first measurements. I did not know enough at the time to interpret these measurements, but there was a reassuring concreteness about them. Alexander's work seemed in many ways so elusive, so hard to grasp, that one yearned for changes such as this—something definite enough to be visible and measurable.

My mind was fairly well made up to go to Alexander before I met Miss Silcox, but my talk with her gave me much confidence, and I was now going to him with hope rather than reluctance.

Chapter 2

MY FIRST SERIES OF LESSONS

Before describing to the reader my first series of lessons with Alexander, it may be helpful for me to attempt to give him an elementary understanding of the HN & B pattern, even at the risk of some oversimplification. If the simplification is so great that the reader cannot understand the explanation, he must turn to Chapter 13 and read a more comprehensive account of the HN & B pattern and to Chapter 15 for a fuller account of *inhibition*.

The pupil attains this new relationship of the head, neck and back through thought. When he is working alone, it is his own unaided conscious thought that brings it about; when he is working with a teacher, it is the association of the teacher's hands and the pupil's thought that brings it about.

The first step in the pattern is *neck free*. This means that the neck becomes progressively freer with each thought that is given to it. Complete freedom of the neck, however, comes only when the condition and functioning of the back has improved.

The second step in the pattern is *head forward* (in relation to the neck) and *up*, as on page 138. On page 139 one sees the head forward in space. There is no ambiguity about the word 'up'; the pupil is to think the head up from the neck after the forward has taken place.

The third step is *back lengthening*. Here the pupil is to think of the back lengthening, including the pelvis as a part of the back, not ending the back at the waist.

The *back widening*: for this step the pupil is to think of the back widening directly after the lengthening. The lengthening and widening must go together. The reader might best be helped to get an idea of the back lengthening and widening by considering these two outlines of skeletal alignment. On page 139 the skeleton is aligned as if the back were shortened and narrowed. The exaggerated curve of the lumbar spine denotes the shortening. The position of the rib cage, which is collapsed, and narrowed in the back and protruding in front, denotes the narrowing. On page 138 the skeleton is aligned as it would be if the back were lengthening and widening. There is no undue curve in the lumbar spine and the rib cage is normally placed, not sticking out in front or narrowing in the back.

This statement is both brief and oversimplified, but it is to be hoped that it will give the reader the beginnings of an understanding of the different steps that make up the HN & B pattern.

Alexander's technique of inhibition must also be described. When Alexander first discovered the new HN & B pattern and tried to maintain it in speaking, he found he could not do so. After much reasoning and experimentation, he finally reached the conclusion that there was an inseparable fusion between the idea of speaking and the body pattern always used in speaking. If he was to get rid of the old body pattern that had caused his voice trouble and substitute the new HN & B pattern when he spoke, he would have to get rid of the idea of speaking! He cut through this seemingly impossible impasse by some brilliant thinking. He 'inhibited' or said 'no' to the idea of speaking, and then focused his mind on each of the component parts of speaking, such as opening his mouth, saying a sound, saying a word, etc. In this way he was able to keep the thought of speaking out of his mind and yet do the things that resulted in speech. In this way, and with severe mental discipline, he was able to maintain the new HN & B pattern when he spoke or recited. This, indeed, is the bare bones of Alexander's technique of 'inhibition'. For a more intelligible and comprehensive account, see Chapter 15. In spite of the obvious limitations of such a summary, the reader may be better equipped to understand those sections of the following chapters which pertain to Alexander's teaching.

In September of 1929, shortly after I returned to London from my visit to the Woods, I had my first interview with F. M. Alexander. I was most deeply curious as to what manner of man I was going to meet. Everything I knew or had heard about him was impressive: the changes in Catherine, Mrs Brown, and Miss Silcox, the praise and admiration expressed by John Dewey in his introductions to Alexander's books ('Admiration,' wrote Dewey, 'in the original sense of wonder'), the willingness of numbers of Americans to cross the ocean each summer so that they might have lessons, the very names of some of his pupils, past and present, such names as Sir Henry Irving, Viola Tree, Matheson Lang, Lady Beerbohm,

Fig. 1. F. M. Alexander in 1941, age 72.

William Temple, Archbishop of Canterbury, J. B. Duke, tobacco magnate, the Earl of Lytton, former Viceroy of India, and James Harvey Robinson.

Alexander must certainly be an outstanding person. Beyond this I did not know what to expect, but I was agog with interest when I stepped into Alexander's teaching room and saw him for the first time. 'So this is the man,' I said to myself. 'How surprising.' His body and his face were a strange contrast, his body being short, slight and incredibly dynamic and youthful. It looked as if it were the body of a man of 20 and had a balanced evenness of development, quite the opposite from what one sees in the pictures of Sandow and other leaders of physical culture systems. His movements too were youthful; he was lithe and extraordinarily graceful. His face, however, was strained. There were no signs of tranquillity there, and he looked all of his 60 years. It was a thin, oval-shaped face with exceptionally alert eyes. They reminded one of the alertness one sees in babies' eyes. At times when he was amused they had a whimsical, elfish look, but at other times they were coldly impersonal. One thing that dumbfounded me was that his face showed no life's experience that I could envy. 'How can this be,' I asked myself, 'when he has done so much for people?'

He was meticulously well dressed, dapper, and slightly theatrical in appearance; a white carnation adorned his buttonhole.

The theatrical element in his appearance was not conducive to inspiring professional confidence; nevertheless, the minute we got on to the professional plane he at once conveyed authority and inspired confidence. I later learned that he did not always do this, and it was fortunate for me that I was a person of no particular prominence. With such people he was often at his worst. He would rattle off the names of his pupils who had titles or other claims to fame and 'show off' generally. But with me in this first interview he was perfectly natural.

He examined me by watching me walk, stand, sit and get up. He placed his hands on me during these activities and noted what was happening. No undressing took place—I discovered later that men pupils never even took off their coats for an examination. I spoke to him about the contrast between his examination and that of the ordinary doctor.

'Certainly,' he said. 'We are after something quite different. In a case like yours, doctors would be interested in the functioning of individual muscles. I do not handle individual muscles. I affect their functioning, of course, but indirectly through the Primary Control.

'I am not interested in the particular manifestation of a pupil's wrongness,' he went on to say. 'I do the same thing for everyone, whether he comes to me with flat feet or nervous tension. I help him to get his Primary Control working again, and when this happens, the pupil will be on the right total pattern and his use and functioning will be at their potential best. A pupil does not have to undress for you to know what his total pattern is.'

During his examination of me he had said, 'Will you please take a step backwards?'

This was the one thing that was almost a physical impossibility for me, and I thought it was almost uncanny that he could discern so immediately this difficulty of mine. He then said, 'I find great fault with your back. With a back like that it is surprising that you walk as well as you do.' The idea that one's walk was bound up with and dependent upon the condition of one's back was quite new to me and I mentioned this to Alexander.

'You will find', he said, 'that as the functioning of your back improves with lessons, your walk too will greatly improve without your feet and legs having been touched.'

Then I brought up another matter that I thought was crucial. 'Mr Alexander,' I said, 'in addition to the destruction in my body caused by polio, I have had tendons transplanted in my left foot, and my right ankle has been immobilized by surgery. Would not this rule out your work for me?'

'On the contrary,' he said. 'This makes it even more important that you be taught to use what you have in the most co-ordinated way possible. When one has had polio, it is as if certain connections in a telephone system have been destroyed. The system will then work in a very helter-skelter way—and so will the body of someone who has had polio. And this, in its turn, brings about increasingly bad co-ordination. Exercises or surgery in a specific part of a harmed body may sometimes cause temporary improvement, but in the long run they are likely to increase the mal-co-ordination of the body as a whole, and this, in time, will affect adversely the specific part. In my experience, mal-co-ordination rather than the initial destruction left by disease is often the primary factor in a person's difficulties and always it is an important contributing factor.'

'But, Mr Alexander,' I said, 'are there not cases where a person's injury is so great, or where surgery has been so drastic, that the Primary Control can no longer be made to work?'

'Yes,' he said, 'there are. I have just had a woman from Boston who has had a very drastic back operation. Her Primary Control will never be able to function again. Also a terrible injury could cause the breakdown of the Primary Control. Such cases, however, are far, far less frequent than people think. My experience has shown me how amazingly the functioning of the Primary Control can improve the condition of persons with very serious injuries.'

Alexander ended our talk by saying that there were indications that I could improve substantially. 'I cannot tell you yet how much improvement you can expect,' he said. 'It will depend upon the extent to which your condition is caused by mal-co-ordination. I think a great deal of it is, but we can only find out about this as we go along.'

These last words of his seemed to me to be both honest and moderate, and they increased my confidence in him.

Happily, Alexander's teaching room did not in any way resemble a treatment room or a doctor's office; if it had, I am quite sure I would never have gone back to him a second time, as the very sight of medical equipment and paraphernalia disturbed and frightened me. The room in which he taught was unmistakably a drawing-room and a very individual one. There was a cheerful fire burning and good antique English furniture about, yet it was not at all like an English drawing-room. It looked as if it belonged to this particular individual and seemed expressive of him. The colour scheme was both interesting and queer. It created a harmony, but it also gave out a mood that was slightly fantastic and unwholesome. The predominant colours were mustard and black, but these, as I remember it, were softened and enhanced by other colour accents. His wife, whose taste in colour he admired very much, was responsible for this colour scheme. Hanging in the double window directly in front of his teaching chair was a very pleasing piece of stained glass. He often advised pupils to look at something pleasing like this while they were working. This bit of stained glass and a cigar box covered in velvet were the only 'professional equipment' Alexander used. The box was helpful in getting a pupil's back in a more vertical position if he was sitting in a chair that had a backward slant.

I went from his room into the office of his secretary, Miss Webb. Here again the room looked more like a sitting-room than an office. It contained an antique desk, a fine oak chest, and a large, comfortable, shabby-looking armchair. There was nothing about the room that was businesslike, clinical, or even efficient, and I liked it very much. Miss Webb herself appealed to me greatly. I felt comfortable with her at once. She was a small, cosy, attractive-looking woman with just the right amount of plumpness. The first remark she made which I remember was that I should not plan to do too much while I was in London as there would be changes in my body which would prove very tiring to me. I found these words delightful.

I talked over the matter of fees with Miss Webb. Alexander's regular fee for a lesson was 3 guineas, or 15 dollars. Mrs Brown had warned me that there was too much vagueness about business arrangements at Ashley Place and that it would be advisable for me to state at the beginning the total amount I could spend on lessons. This I did. I told Miss Webb I could spend 300 dollars on lessons at this time. I did not know if Alexander would even take me for this amount, and if so how many lessons I could expect to get. Yes, he would take me,

Miss Webb said; the autumn was his slack season. But I could not find out definitely how many lessons I would have. I deplored this, although as it turned out Alexander was generous with me. I had a lesson every day, five days a week, for two months.

In my first lesson I understood very little, if anything, of what Alexander was doing or what he wanted me to do. He used his hands on me a great deal and in the most subtle, delicate way, making what seemed to be minute, infinitesimal changes in my body in the region of my head, neck and back. After a short interval, however, these tiny adjustments would add up to a substantial change which would often feel uncomfortable and unfamiliar. And so he went on. He worked on me while I was sitting in a chair and while I was standing up, and he also, with his hands on my head, took me in and out of a chair. At the end of the lesson he walked me around the room with his hands on my head, and I felt as light as air. But even this was not a pleasant feeling, as I felt shaky and uncontrolled. My old equilibrium was gone and my legs seemed to dangle, Alexander's hands were amazing; sometimes they almost seemed to be doing nothing at all or something that was so imperceptible that it passed for nothing. Yet in reality they were always building up and strengthening a new HN & B pattern, thus producing fundamental changes in my body. It was as if my body was put on a different control. His hands impressed me so much that I thought over the qualities they possessed. They were dry, cool, light and impersonal, but above all they had a quality that gave me complete confidence and made me want to go with them.

While Alexander worked on me with his hands, he told me to 'order' or 'direct' my neck to relax, my head to go forward and up, and my back to lengthen and widen. He said these words as if he were repeating a formula, and they had no meaning to me. I did not know that to 'order' or 'direct' meant to think. I did not know that head forward meant forward in relation to the neck. Then he took me in and out of a chair a number of times, and he told me each time that I got up or sat down to 'inhibit' or say 'no' so that I could get rid of my old pattern of getting up or sitting down. There were several other phrases about 'inhibition' which he used as well, but not a thing he said had any meaning for me, and I was plunged into dire confusion. I had no notion that there was a fusion between my idea of sitting down and my old muscular pattern of sitting down, so that I would have to inhibit the idea to get rid of the faulty pattern. Even if I had understood this, I would never have been able to apply this difficult technique so quickly. I was to say, 'No, I am not going to get up,' knowing that I'd be taken up in about five seconds. It seemed wholly unintelligible and like some trick or hocus pocus. What *did* the man mean? I was completely at sea. But he expected very little of me that first lesson and I believed that understanding would come as I had more work. I was spending one more night with my friend at her hotel, and I returned there after my lesson. I felt rather sickish and as if I wanted to lie down, and my neck felt sore and twisted. I did lie down for the whole evening. I got up for dinner but went back to bed again immediately afterwards. The next morning I felt somewhat better but still rather queer and uncomfortable.

From then on I had a lesson every day, five days a week, for two months. My body often felt unfamiliar and uncomfortable but I never again felt as uncomfortable as I had after my first lesson. Although I did not understand Alexander's instructions for a wearyingly long time, the uniqueness of his work became clearer to me each day. I saw that the new HN & B pattern he had discovered was its foundation stone and that anyone desiring to understand the work is called upon to reorient himself to a new outlook, namely, that of a basic body pattern being the decisive factor in overcoming both general and specific defects.

Just as the first students of Freud had to reorient themselves in regard to the unconscious, and the first students of Einstein had to reorient themselves in regard to relativity, so the Alexander student must reorient himself in regard to the HN & B pattern. This cannot be too often reiterated. The whole purpose of a lesson was to get this HN & B pattern functioning as strongly as possible and to maintain this functioning while the pupil engaged in everyday activities such as sitting down, getting up, moving backwards and forwards from the hips while sitting in a chair, walking, speaking, etc., and while this may sound misleadingly easy (partly because the words used in describing it are simple and familiar), it does in fact require the greatest discipline and skill. The pupil is beset by unfamiliar and misleading sensations which intrude upon his thinking. Sometimes he has no sensation at all, which disturbs him even more, as it has been bred into him that no change can take place without effortful 'muscular doing'.

But even the beginner has rewards. I was often conscious of an unfamiliar control taking charge of my body, enabling me to have more movement in my knees and ankles and in general to move with more power and grace. As Sir Stafford Cripps expressed it: 'Instead of feeling one's body to be an aggregation of ill-fitting parts . . . the body becomes a co-ordinated and living whole.' Nor were my rewards limited to the physical.

I enjoyed a clarity of thought and a tranquillity of emotions never before experienced.

After each lesson I found walking much easier. One day I had a wonderful new feeling as I walked down the hall at Ashley Place. I tried to accentuate this feeling, thinking I was doing something to aid my new walk. As I pranced along, A. R. Alexander, F. M.'s brother, appeared in the hall and started swearing at me. He had a rich vocabulary, but most often his swearing signified regard or interest. He made it clear to me that I was just feeling something out, and instead of strengthening my new condition I was destroying it. This condition could not be obtained through feeling but only by the bringing to life of the HN & B pattern through conscious thought.

It was my first personal experience of Alexander's discovery that our 'feelings' were unreliable. Here I was doing harmful things to myself and completely unaware of it.

One other thing that took place in this first series of lessons was an emotional scene. I was standing up and F. M. asked me to give the series of head, neck and back orders, and to 'come back to his hands'. I did not know whether he meant me to step back, to allow myself to fall back, to think the back back, or what. There were several alternatives as to what he might mean. To F. M., however, the words 'come back to my hands' meant exactly one thing: what he intended them to mean. It was like the remark of Humpty Dumpty's: 'When I use a word, it means just what I choose it to mean, neither more nor less.' Since I simply didn't know what F. M. meant me to do, I wavered, hesitated and tried one possible alternative after the other. We had reached a total impasse. I got more and more frantic, and he got more and more furious. Finally he burst out, 'You make me feel like a fool.' It surprised me that this should be his main concern and the cause of his anger.

It both upset and enraged him when he could not get a point over to a pupil, and yet verbally he did nothing about it. He kept reiterating his original words and never attempted a different phrasing. In this instance he kept on saying, 'Come back to my hands,' making no effort to elucidate what he meant or to clear up the ambiguity. His was the Humpty Dumpty outlook: a word meant just what he intended it to mean. If the pupil didn't understand, there was a total impasse. Alexander never seemed to envisage the different shades of meaning in a phrase or sentence.

After I had been having lessons for about two weeks, my back began to ache frequently and severely. Sometimes it ached almost continuously. It was here that I had my first and only period of fear. I remembered an orthopaedic doctor saying, 'Well, thank goodness her back is rigid. If that rigidity went, I don't know what would happen.' And I thought to myself, 'Here you are, going to a layman, who, so far as New Orleans is concerned, is totally unknown. You don't know what is happening, really, and whether it is dangerous or not.' I decided to have a look at my back in the mirror and was somewhat amazed as well as delighted by what I saw. My back was much straighter than it had been and appeared longer; and although my shoulders (one of which was very over-developed while the other was under-developed) were still structurally very different, the difference was not so noticeable. The shoulders were lower and wider than they had been, and the over-developed one did not hunch up with every movement I made, as it had previously. This look in the mirror reassured me a great deal; and then other things began to reassure me, too.

I was in the National Gallery one afternoon and looked at my watch. 'This is impossible,' I said to myself, and looked at it again. But it was a fact. I had been there for two and a half hours, and my feet were not tired. Compared to what I was usually able to do, this was quite fantastic. Ordinarily my feet would have been troubling me in thirty minutes.

Then, too, other people began to notice the change. I went to tea one afternoon with a distant cousin. I was not very close to her, and so I had not told her I was going to Alexander. Although she seemed slightly hesitant and embarrassed about mentioning any improvement at first, she was finally unable to restrain herself. She said that my walk had improved immensely and that my whole frame had come into line and was poised differently.

When I saw my half-sister again, the change that struck her as foremost was the muscular development in my calves. They had previously presented a wasted, withered appearance, particularly the calf in the right leg.

An orthopaedic doctor once told me that I had no calf muscles and that the withered appearance of my calves was due to muscle wastage. In two months of lessons with Alexander my calves developed markedly, and they took on the look of legs that were used and developed—not normally developed yet but still developed—the withered unused look that they had previously had was gone. I should add that at no time in this series of lessons did Alexander touch my feet or legs or ask me to do anything about them. There was something else that I myself noticed. Whenever I had debated at college, or presided over a meeting, or gone to a large party, I had been unpleasantly conscious of my arms. They had always seemed to hang in the wrong place, and I never knew what to do with them and was, therefore, uncomfortable and nervous. During this first session of lessons with Alexander I went to a cocktail party and suddenly realized, as I was entering the room, that I had a great sense of ease and assurance. Afterwards I remembered that I had not been aware of my arms at all. I looked at them in the mirror and noticed they were slung in a different way, the backs of the hands tending to fall outwards (as in fig. 19).* Before, the insides of my hands were tending to fall inwards. Later on in the training course I was to learn that the pattern of the back determines the placement of the arms in their sockets, but at this time I knew nothing except that my arms were slung differently and they did not obtrude themselves upon my notice.

I now had a degree of tranquillity that I had not experienced since I had had infantile paralysis, and together with that and possibly part of it, some increase in my ability to meet difficult situations.

Although my first series of lessons with Alexander brought about a great change, yet from day to day one never realized this, as changes took place quietly, gradually, often imperceptibly and only from time to time could one be conscious of a basic shift and improvement. These heartening improvements made one think how incredibly expert Alexander's hands must be when he could bring such things about in a fairly short time and when he had difficulty in getting over to the pupil through words what he wanted the pupil to do. It made one think afresh of the extraordinary power of the HN & B pattern. It seemed fantastic and sad that this factor, which had so powerfully affected my health and well being, was unknown and unused in the therapies of today.

As I could not yet carry on the work by myself, I was fearful that some of my gains might be lost. I believed, hopefully, that the whole problem of understanding would be solved by taking a sufficient number of lessons. The question was how to get them. Individual lessons were expensive, and a great number of them would have been quite beyond my means.

---

* See picture of knight in armour illustrating how the arms should be placed in their sockets, p. 140.

But Alexander was talking at this time of starting his first teacher's training course, and I thought this might be the answer to my problem. He spoke as if this course might start any time within the next six months, although it did not actually start for two years. But I wanted time, since if I came back to London I would need to earn some money, and I must also think over the various problems involved in such a step.

And so my first series of lessons ended, and I returned to the United States.

Chapter 3

EARLY DAYS OF THE TRAINING COURSE

After my first series of lessons with Alexander had ended in the autumn of 1929, I returned to the United States and stayed there for two years. During this time I earned some money, and I thought over the various points that it seemed necessary to consider before making my final decision as to whether or not I would train as a teacher in this new work.

No training course had ever been held, so it was an open question whether teachers could be trained to teach. Perhaps this skill was not transmissible but was the individual gift of two men—F. M. Alexander and his brother, A. R. Alexander.

Then, too, the course would take three years and would cost two thousand five hundred dollars. At the end of that time one would be in a pioneer profession known to only a handful of Americans and unprotected by any recognized organization. On the other hand, it would be a great adventure; a gamble, yes, and probably very hard going, but at all times an adventure. I felt also that what I did in the work would be superlatively worthwhile and that I would enjoy doing it.

So in spite of the risk involved and the expense, I was favourably inclined towards joining the course. I believe, however, that the strongest factor influencing my decision to do this was to get help for myself. So when the course started in London in February 1931, I was there.

It was a bleak, chilly day such as only a London February can produce when seven of us enrolled in F. Matthias Alexander's first training course for teachers. We felt it to be an important occasion, both in our own lives and in the history of Alexander's work, and so indeed it was.

Our number gradually increased to twelve. We were a 'mixed grill' in regard to age, nationality, reasons for entering the course, education, and environment. Ages ranged from

Fig. 2 On the stairs of 16 Ashley Place in 1931: Erika Schumann (Whittaker), Margaret Goldie, Jean MacInnes, Marjorie Barstow, Irene Stewart, Gurney MacInnes, (in front) Lulie Westfeldt, Maxwell Alexander, George Trevelyan. All were members of the first training with the exception of Max (son of A. R. Alexander) who joined in 1934. Catherine Merrick (Wielopolska) also started in 1931. Patrick Macdonald joined in 1932. Marjory Mechin (Barlow) and Charles Neil joined in 1933.

16 to 35 years; I was the oldest. Of the final twelve, three came from the United States, two from Scotland, and the rest from England. Eight of those who came into the course had had private lessons and fully appreciated what the work could do. They chose consciously and eagerly to make it their profession. One was pressed into the work by his family some-

what against his will, and one other had no clear-cut reason that could be discovered for choosing the work as her profession. The remaining two, a young Scot and myself, came in mainly because of personal handicaps. He had appalling attacks of asthma; nothing had helped him; and his disability so interfered with his life and education that his father, who was a poor man, had made a desperate effort and had sent him to Alexander. A small percentage had somewhat scant education; most of us had average good English or Scottish educations; and six of us had university degrees. We Americans had B.A. degrees from different universities, and three of the Englishmen were Cambridge graduates.

The only qualifications required for the members of our group were the ability to pay the five-hundred-pound fee and our willingness to pledge ourselves to stay for three years and not to teach anyone during that time. F. M., however, was free to put us out at any time during the three years, should it seem to him advisable to do so.

We were called 'students' to distinguish us from private pupils.

We had to have the same work as private pupils before we could begin to use our hands on others, as the teacher's hands must have qualities that only good use and co-ordination can give them, that is, strength without tension and a superlatively high degree of sensitivity.

The course met five days a week for nine months in the year. F. M. would work with us from ten to twelve in the morning, and often his brother A. R., until he went to the United States in 1933, would work with us too.

The time for the class was two hours, whether there were seven of us or twelve of us, and whether we had two teachers or one, so that the amount of individual teaching and attention that we had daily varied from fifteen minutes to half an hour.

We used A. R. Alexander's teaching room, as it was big enough for the twelve of us. We would stand in a circle. There were a few chairs in the room, and a huge sofa covered in black sateen so that when any of us got tired we could sit down and rest and watch what was going on.

During the winter months a coal fire always burned in the grate and two of the American students (a friend and myself) commandeered places on either side of this fire permanently and forever. Fortunately the third American did not compete with us for these places. She outdid the hardy English in stoical practices.

I can see us now, standing in a circle, a fire burning, and the two Americans claiming squatter's rights in the places of greatest warmth, the men wearing grey flannel trousers and sports coats, and the women wearing tweed skirts and somewhat drab-looking sweaters. As the weather grew colder, the women would add on additional layers of sweaters and cardigans.

F. M. would make the rounds, working on each one of us. The pupil would be giving the sequence of thoughts or 'orders' that would cause the HN & B pattern to function. When F. M. put his hands on a student, he would, in an infinitely subtle and delicate way, free the student's neck, take his head forward and up, lengthen and widen his back. The student's thought and the teacher's hand would thus work in association to establish the new HN & B pattern.

The student might be in various positions at the beginning of a lesson: sitting, standing, or lying; or he might be in what we called the 'monkey position' where the knees were forward and apart and the torso inclined at a forward angle.

After the HN & B pattern had been well established, simple everyday movements would be attempted, such as walking, sitting down, getting up, and moving backwards and forwards from the hips while sitting. To maintain the HN & B pattern in an activity, F. M.'s technique of inhibition had to be used (see Chapter 15).

We also learned a good deal from watching F. M. work on the other students. We saw the transforming difference that the HN & B pattern made not only in the student's stance, contours, alignment, grace and control of movement, but also, strangely enough, in the significance of the impression he made as a person. 'Every mental order we project has a discernible physical aspect—a concreteness,' F. M. had said, and this we were now seeing daily.

Of course, the all-important work time was our session with F. M. in the morning, but we also worked alone for three or four hours in the afternoon using our hands on each other. If F. M. were free, which happened about once or twice a month, and we were in a dilemma, he would come in for a few minutes and try to clear up the difficulty. In the afternoon we worked in what was called the 'Student's Room'. It was very small and was so inadequate for our needs that we had to form groups and work in different places, one group remaining in the Students' Room and the other groups working in the flats, lodgings, or houses belonging to the various students. This dividing up into groups and each group working in a different place proved to be a great help to me later on when I felt that I needed to protect myself from the unsupervised hands of beginners.

Disturbances came in time, but it would have been exceedingly difficult to have been disturbed by anything in those early days of the training course. They were halcyon ones for all of us. We were embarked together on an exciting journey. We were learning something new—which is always fun—and as we were beginners we were not worried over our progress. We also thought that what we were learning was glorious, and that we were lucky to be able to choose such a work. And if that were not enough, our daily life was both gay and interesting.

I think that this was so for all the students, but for a foreigner like myself, where everything was novel and unfamiliar, there was an added element of interest and delight. That first winter I treasured even the London fogs: there was always a feeling of adventure about them—how was one going to get home, for example—and then they did really bear out what the books said; they had the visually impenetrable quality of pea soup. But it was not only London that I loved with its Inns of Court, its Temple Round Church, its Westminster Bridge—it was the length and breadth of England.

Because my British colleagues were interested in and

curious about us Americans, I did not have to go through the usual long period of waiting and being looked over before their doors were opened to me. Their doors were opened from the beginning, in warm-hearted hospitality, so that in my holidays I had the rare opportunity of visiting many different kinds of homes, from a 'stately home of England' full of beautiful things and so large that I needed help that first evening in finding my way about, to a simple Scotch cottage with a kitchen living-room where we played poker every evening, drank very strong tea, and occasionally ate 'blood pudding' (an unexpectedly good dish) for supper. My colleagues' hospitality also meant that I travelled from the friendly rolling downs of the south to the wilder moors of the north, sometimes bleak and sometimes heather-covered, but always beautiful. Small wonder that no problems or disturbing thoughts could enter my mind at this time. We were all starry-eyed, and I possibly even more so than the rest as I had the most to gain from this work. We felt that we were bound together in a unique enterprise and that we were the *élite* of all the earth. We admired F. M. uncritically and wholeheartedly, and he basked in our admiration. We were indeed a mutual admiration society with everyone admiring himself and everyone else and F. M. most of all. We began to have grave doubts about the other human beings outside our orbits.

F. M. had his own particular way of expressing his commiseration for these unfortunates. Often in class he would look out of the window and remark on the passers-by. 'Look at that man,' he would say, 'he's a wreck,' or 'See that woman—poor thing, she's mad, completely mad.'

But as our doubts about the rest of the world increased, a few of us began to perceive how benighted, happily benighted, we all were, and to regain at least an intermittent connection with our reason.

At this time all of us felt that *'der Tag'*—the day when Alexander's work would be universally recognized, appreciated, and used—was just around the corner. To our inexperienced eyes there were sound grounds for this. A number of very promising opportunities seemed on the verge of coming to a head, and there were people of fine quality impressed by the work and anxious to promote it. Anthony Ludovici, an author and pupil of F. M.'s, was going to write a book about the work; Miss Lawrence, the former head of the Froebel

Fig. 3. F. M. Alexander on holiday in Bognor Regis, Sussex, 1939.

Institute, was planning to buy a house and start an Alexander school for small children. There was also a devoted group of doctors coming for lessons and sending their patients, writing pamphlets and articles in medical journals, addressing medical meetings, and making every possible effort to bring Alexander's work to the attention of the medical profession and promote its sound establishment and growth.

Still another opportunity that seemed most promising was the interest of an American foundation in the work. F. M. had been talking about this for some time. He said the foundation wished to donate money to further the work, in what way we did not know. He said it was a great opportunity and that he might have to go to the United States to see the people there and work out plans. He spoke vaguely about it, and his vagueness increased, but we did not recognize this as a danger signal, for we did not at this time know that F. M. had a way of killing an opportunity, although in the beginning he apparently accepted it and rejoiced in it. His rejoicing had every indication of being genuine, and I believe that in some strange way it was. When a promising opportunity came, he would suggest that we all drink sherry together in honour of the occasion, but shortly after that a veil—an ever-thickening veil—would be dropped over the whole affair, and it would be practically impossible to find out what had actually happened, except we would finally know that in some way the opportunity no longer existed. But as we did not yet know the fate of 'opportunities', we continued to be most hopeful as to the future of the work and continued having a wonderfully good time.

F. M. was a wit and classes were vastly entertaining. A great deal of his talk consisted of funny stories, jokes, and repartee. And, of course, he talked about horse races, the prospects in the coming Derby, the hazards of Tattenham Corner, and so forth. But what he loved most to tell us about were his early days in London with theatre people. In about 1904, when he first came to London, Dr Robert Spicer, a throat specialist, had been influential in getting him work to do in a number of London theatres. He taught the actors and actresses his work

Fig. 4. On the Verandah at Penhill, *c.* 1931: F. M. Alexander, Catherine Merrick (Wielopolska), Ethel Webb, George Trevelyan, A. R. Alexander, Erika Schumann (Whittaker), Lulie Westfeldt, Gurney MacInnes, Marjorie Barstow.

to enable them to handle their problems of voice production and movement to the best advantage. It was during this period that F. M. taught Sir Henry Irving, Viola Tree, Sarah Brooks, Matheson Lang and others. Matheson Lang still came to F. M. for an occasional lesson at the time of our training course. I remember F. M. bringing him in to see us one day.

What F. M. most enjoyed telling us about when he recalled those early days was the play *When Knights Were Bold* and his work with Jimmy Welch, the leading comedian. He thought the play superb. It appealed to his particular brand of humour. Jimmy Welch had collapsed after the first night of the play, and F. M.'s job was to get him in such shape that he could carry on. Alexander succeeded in doing this and the play had a long run with Jimmy at the helm.

We heard much about these days in our morning hours of

work, and F. M. always seemed renewed and invigorated when he talked of them. We were getting our first introduction to the passionate attachment he had for the theatre, though perhaps one should add, the theatre when he himself was connected with it.

Once we all went to see *The Mikado* together. The next day I remember F. M.'s pointing out how 'weak-kneed' (literally) they all looked when they bent their knees. Then he bent his knees to demonstrate the strength and significance shown in what he called 'a proper knee thrust' (which takes place when the new HN & B pattern is functioning). The difference between F. M.'s knee thrust, as he showed it to us that day, and the bent knees of the actors we had seen the evening before was truly dramatic. Whenever he demonstrated a point like this, one thought of him as a great master, as the action of his body illustrated with complete perfection the idea he wanted to get across. (See the knee thrust of the Etruscan warrior, fig. 21, page 143).

Another time we all went together to see Robert Donat in a movie (Donat had had lessons from F. M.). In the opening scene Donat was sitting in an English railway coach. One knew he was going to get up soon, and one had a feeling of intense suspense (quite as great as when watching a murder mystery): is he or is he not going to 'retract the head upon the neck' when he gets up? Alas! he did retract his head, but only slightly.

On special occasions such as the end of a term, F. M. would have us all down to his country house, Penhill, in Sidcup, Kent, and after we had eaten and settled down for the evening we would cry, 'F. M.! F. M.! *The Billiard Marker*, F. M.! *The Race*, F. M.!' Always we would ask for Australian tales, and when he recited these he was marvellous. Indeed, whenever he recited Australian tales we would be sitting on the edges of our chairs, practically falling off, although we knew every word of each of them and exactly what was coming next. However, after a bit of this—an all too short amount— another trend would start. F. M. would start picking out the things he liked. The weightier bits of Shakespeare would come in. (We did not in the least like the way he recited them.) Then a particular favourite of his called *Napoleon*, which we considered ghastly, would always be the climax. It ended with 'I would rather be a peasant sitting in my humble cottage, my wife by my side and our child upon my knees—than Napoleon the Great.' At the end his voice would shake and quaver. There was never any staving off *Napoleon*. It always crept in, no matter what he started off with or how vociferously we called for the ones we liked.

There was no one who could be better company than F. M. in a witty, light way. His words were not scintillating, but his way of saying them, his gestures, his mannerisms, were. Many of us felt after hearing him recite his Australian tales that he could have made a fortune any day as a comedian. I, for one, never doubted it. Where his own particular brand of humour was concerned, he was a great artist and irresistible.

In these early days of the course, our relationship with him was the happiest. Nothing serious had come up; no testing had taken place; no problems were on the horizon. He greatly enjoyed his band of disciples who were also his audience, his acquiescing and admiring audience.

Chapter 4

GRADUAL CHANGE IN MY OUTLOOK ON ALEXANDER

As the training course progressed I learned to know more and more about Alexander the man—through the incidents of our daily life together and from what he told us about his early days in a pioneer environment. My euphoric dream was not yet over, but my increasing knowledge of him as a human being with difficulties and limitations like everyone else, and indeed in a greater degree than most people, weakened the dream somewhat and marked the beginning of the end. It was this knowledge of the man that enabled me to see what caused him to handle his work the way he did, spreading its fame on the one hand, impeding its growth and establishment on the other. No one can understand the position of the work in the world today without knowing the man, his quirks and psychological difficulties.

My first picture of F. M.'s daily life and interests was given me by our visits to Penhill. Penhill was near enough to London for F. M. to commute daily. He kept a gardener called Rose and a woman who looked after the house and cooked for him. Outside, the house was pleasing, unpretentious and comfortable. Inside, one saw again the strange colour schemes of Mrs Alexander. They did not look so well at Penhill as they did at Ashley Place. They seemed less suitable for a simple country house, too sophisticated and somewhat unwholesome. When, later on, Alexander's little school for children was moved to Penhill, various people remarked on the possible effect such a colour scheme would have on small children.

On his Sundays at Penhill F. M. would take a horseback ride. This was his one recreation. He liked Penhill and enjoyed being there, but it was not an absorbing interest to him and he did not potter around doing things about the place himself as many an Englishman is apt to do on his country place. F. M., throughout his life, had exactly three interests apart from his work: food, horse racing and acting. The first two of these were born of his frontier environment.

In describing his early days, Alexander told us what an important part good food and its proper preparation played in the life of his family. They would take any amount of trouble about it. They would kill one of their own lambs, for instance, hang it just the right number of days, and then at the strategic moment cut slits in the carcass and pour in red wine for flavouring. The preparation of even a minor dish had to be just right. (During the training-course days some of us once went together in a party to the Derby, and the elaborate ritual the Alexander brothers advised us to go through in order to make tea and put it in thermos bottles was amazing.) The subject of food would frequently come into the training course. He would talk about the relative merits of well-known London restaurant and tell us what we were going to have for our summer term dinner at Penhill. In the early days of the course we had things like a saddle of mutton and a magnum of champagne, but with the years our fare deteriorated until in the end it resembled Sunday School box suppers. Attending horse races was the favourite sport of his youth and everyone bet on these races. Horse racing continued to be a passion with him although at this time he rarely had the leisure to go to the races. On the few occasions when he did go, he would appear, looking very dapper indeed and like an actor, in what we rather affectionately called the 'grasshopper' suit—a grey morning coat and matching trousers and a grey top hat. F. M. liked us to speak of his grasshopper suit, and for our benefit he moved quite like a grasshopper when he had it on.

Betting on horse races, however, continued to be his passion; in fact, it was the greatest outlet of his life. F. M. made no secret of his interest in betting, but the details and the extent of it we found out only in the course of time. When I did find out, I was staggered. Later on I became more tolerant, realizing that what to an American might seem an obsession could to a pioneer Australian be in the natural order of things, and also realizing that he very much needed an outlet from his work since so few things interested him. Be that as it may, the fact was that F. M. had a number of betting accounts under different names, and he placed a bet *every half hour* of every working day.

There was always someone at 16 Ashley Place who was trained to place these bets for him. At first it was his man, Leonard, who did odd jobs for him at Ashley Place, and then when Leonard left it was one of his best teachers. She had to interrupt the lesson she was giving to go and phone in the bet. When A. R. Alexander came back from America in summers, an extra telephone was installed at 16 Ashley Place so that he could place his bets. To judge by these two men, it was indeed an Australian custom.

It is interesting to note that Alexander never mentioned any discussions of ideas as taking place in his youth. Neither he nor his family were given to theories or abstract speculation, their interests being centred on simple concrete things. His own interest in acting was the one exception to this.

Although he spent most of his nights at Penhill, he had a bedroom at Ashley Place which he could use if he wanted to stay in town. He went about town very little, however. He never went to hear music or to the theatre, for it seemed to be not so much the theatre that he loved but his dream of himself as a Shakespearean actor. Sometimes he would go to the Cafe Royal for a good dinner; this was one of his favourite places. He very seldom dined with friends, and when he did there was usually a professional angle to it.

There were frequent periods in the training course when F. M. was extremely bored. Then we would put our heads together and try to think of things we could suggest or ask that would arouse his interest again. It was a shock to discover that F. M. could get bored teaching—especially teaching us, the future custodians of his work. It is true that his time was almost entirely taken up with his work and it is hard for anyone to be exclusively occupied with one sort of occupation and remain alert and creative in it, unless it corresponds to his own inner needs and desires. We had assumed that F. M.'s work did correspond to his own inner needs and desires, but later on I recognized that it was another emotional urge that had sustained him in his search, a search which lasted nine years and which was so difficult that several times he thought he had reached the end of his tether. It was because he hoped to be a great actor that he went through all this. When the training course was rehearsing *The Merchant of Venice* I saw at first hand the almost alarming strength of his urge to be an actor.

But there was perhaps another reason why he became bored when teaching his students, and it was one which I was loath to consider. A colleague expressed it when she said, 'A part of him doesn't care whether we learn or not, or doesn't believe we can learn. He was pressed into starting a training course by influential people who wanted his work to live, so he said to himself, "All right, I'll have a training course, but I doubt if any of my students will really master my technique".' I felt that there was truth in what my colleague said, though I was reluctant to admit it. Once later on when we asked him to explain to us what he was doing when he put is hand on the floating ribs of a pupil and made an infinitesimal movement, he looked at us with twinkling eyes and said, 'Ah, that is a bag of tricks,' and told us nothing. It was as if he thought that this was something too complicated for us to grasp.

There were some aspects of his work, however, that yielded him great satisfaction: his own extraordinary ability to bring about changes in a pupil, and the gratitude and admiration that his professional achievements brought him.

Near the end of our first year we learned something about F. M.'s family life and the relationship he had with his wife and his adopted daughter, Peggy. He and his wife and Peggy had lived together at Penhill, but shortly before the training course started Mrs Alexander had become ill, and she and Peggy were now staying in a flat at Maida Vale. We students never saw Mrs Alexander. She had originally been an actress, 'not of the top rank', our informants who were old pupils

Fig. 5. F. M. Alexander and his wife, Edith Mary. They married in 1914.

said. Some of them told us that when Mrs Alexander was still living at Penhill F. M. would occasionally ask them there to Sunday dinner. They described her as theatrical in appearance, peculiar and unfriendly. While she did not take much part in the conversation, she always managed to convey the fact that she was wholly antagonistic to F. M.'s work. Indeed, she had decreed that he never give lessons to Peggy. In this matter, which must have meant a great deal to F. M. as he adored Peggy, he did not take the position of master in his own household. Everyone, however, pupils, friends, secretary, was united in saying that F. M. always behaved towards his wife in the most exemplary way. He was kind, considerate, and when there were things he admired about her, such as her colour sense, he never failed to express his admiration. One got the feeling from those who were close to him that he must have had a good deal to put up with, but he did put up with it, with a good grace, and continued to do so until her death. As someone said, in the matter of his marriage he showed <u>conscious control to the</u> nth degree. Indeed, he showed qualities that were even more admirable than control: extraordinary patience, understanding, and forbearance. Many men would have become embittered by such a wife. Think of what her unconcealed antagonism to his work must have meant to him! Yet he never betrayed the slightest trace of bitterness and always spoke of Mrs Alexander in a genuinely pleasant, nice way.

His relationship with Peggy seemed ideal. She was about eleven years old at that time. He may have spoiled her, but one would have difficulty in finding any other grounds for criticism. She came to Ashley Place quite often. The way she and F. M. looked at each other and the tones of their voices when they spoke to each other expressed a relationship of deep trust and love. She called him 'Daddy' and he called her 'Pet'. She went away with him on his holiday every year. This relationship with her seemed to be the only deep and satisfying human contact that F. M. had at that time, and she brought out a tenderness and affection in him that were not often seen.

All that I was now learning about the man gave me insight into the difficulties that I was soon to meet in the training course. Indeed, some of them had already occurred, but I was still so bound up in a dream that I had given them no ear.

Now, however, just before our first long holiday in August 1931, a problem that I had sensed from the beginning came to a head and I found myself utterly discouraged. Although I had come the previous March and had had a lesson every day, I still did not understand Alexander's initial instructions, nor did I know how to carry on the work by myself. Questions were not only not answered but were looked on as symptoms of bad use, and one was 'reassured' by being told that as one's use grew better one would stop asking those things. This was the attitude one met in F. M., his brother A. R., and his secretary.

I was treated, and saw others treated, kindly and indulgently, but as if we were going through a stage of adolescence— 'the question period.' They'll get over that when their conditions change . . . F. M.'s secretary often expressed it in just this way.

In this instance, on the eve of the August holiday, I voiced my depression and discouragement. They were quite kind to me; someone, the secretary, I think, said to come along—she would give me a 'turn' (this is the term we used for lessons). But no one behaved as if I had a legitimate problem which should be met. My first reaction to all this was to wonder if I were really below par mentally. Maybe I had to understand something like the 'categorical imperative' or worse, and I just wasn't up to it. For comfort I reviewed my academic career. I had won a scholarship bracelet offered one term by my fraternity. I had even been elected to Phi Beta Kappa— which ought to be some kind of a guarantee that I wasn't actually below par—so I gradually came to my senses, and, feeling reassured as to my own mental capacity, I began to see that the fault lay with F. M. rather than myself. This was a real landmark in my outlook on Alexander. The dream had faded, the hero-image had fallen off its pedestal, and now I was looking at a man. A man indeed, whose inability to explain verbally what he meant was keeping his pupils from learning the first rudiments of his work. My problem was a representative one and not individual to me. Colleagues in the training course, as well as private pupils who had had a great deal of work, were going around in a fog, not knowing how to carry on the work by themselves and doing some quite wrong things, so that most often they were destroying some of the benefits they had received.

I had assumed that other pupils who did not understand what Alexander meant at least *knew* they did not understand. But as I talked to more and more of them, I found out that this was not so. I remember asking one young man who habitually carried his head and neck forward and down in a rather marked fashion (his interpretation of 'forward' being forward in space) if he did not think that Alexander's inability to explain what he meant to a pupil was not a serious impediment to the growth of his work. 'Why, no,' the young man said. 'I always knew what he meant.' This was true of many people; they believed in a confused sort of way that they knew what Alexander meant and went ahead doing the wrong thing.

But there were also people who knew they were confused and uncertain as to how to carry out Alexander's instructions. One woman was contracting her jaw (like an old-time West Pointer) and holding her chin down. Although this procedure had stiffened and raised her chest and narrowed her upper back, it was her interpretation of what Alexander meant by 'head forward'. Unlike the young man, however, she was not happy about what she was doing, and she had no certainty that it was what Alexander meant by 'forward'.

'Why', the reader may say, 'did you not ask him what he meant?' One would have to know F. M. to understand why not. You simply did not get what you needed when you asked him. The answer didn't meet the question and often mystified you further. If questions were pressed, he would get irritated and behave as though he felt himself persecuted. Always at first new pupils would be inflamed with enthusiasm. Then confusion and doubt would come to them. Ultimately, when they found that they could not keep the work going themselves, they were disappointed. Some pupils who had money and could get to F. M. kept on coming to him constantly. But the rank and file could not afford to do this. I resolved then that if I became a teacher I would make every effort to make the work more intelligible to pupils. I believed this could be done.

Alexander always passed off his ineptness with words by saying that his work was a sensory experience and as such could not be described or communicated in words. What he said was true, but in connection with his initial instructions to pupils it was beside the point; for here the teacher's problem is not to describe an experience but to enable the pupil to follow certain procedures that will result in his having an experience. To do this the teacher's task is to describe the *procedures* (not the experience) in intelligible words. This is not impossible. Many teachers have been doing this for years now, and their pupils have gained an understanding and independence that in my early days in the work was completely unknown.

Alexander's initial instructions of 'direct the neck to relax, the head to go forward and up, the back to lengthen and widen' badly needed some elucidation. What form of activity did the words 'direct' or 'order' indicate, for example? Did they mean 'thinking' or 'doing' or some unknown activity mid-way between the two which the unhappy pupil would try to discover by using the method of trial and error? Also, what did the words 'head forward' mean? They might have several meanings—the pupil unaided would have small chance of guessing the right one (which is forward in relation to the neck).

This lack of communication between F. M. and his pupils on elmentary procedures has, I believe, been a large factor holding back the spread of his work. One of the hardest experiences that any pupil could have, and many had it, was the realization that his own efforts to keep the work going were proving harmful rather than helpful.

Shortly after I had realized Alexander's ineptness with words he came into the classroom one morning and said exultingly, 'I can get it now in spite of them.' He said that his hands were now sufficiently skilled to get the new HN & B pattern going without the pupil's help. He spoke as if a great burden had been lifted from him, as if he were freed from the frustrating struggle of trying to get the pupil to understand him. While he seemed to feel morally responsible for changing a pupil's condition, he did not feel responsible for communicating with the pupil or for giving him understanding. From that day I never saw F. M. have another emotional scene with a pupil. Scenes were now unnecessary.

By this time my hero-image had toppled, and I was inclined to be critical of many things which in the first part of the course I had let pass without notice.

One of our group was living on two pounds a week, which covered everything, including rather heavy expenses home in the holidays. Even in the year 1931 this sum seemed unhealthily low, and this colleague was far from robust. I kept wishing that Alexander would be concerned about this and that some plan could be worked out for needy students to receive help from the Alexander Trust Fund. For Alexander's work to become a respected profession, it seemed to me basic that he be concerned both with obtaining good teacher material and with seeing that his students worked under healthful conditions. It was difficult to see why, if no initial qualifications of students were required, a training course could not have been started much earlier. What was Alexander waiting for? Could it be that he was not anxious to start a training course? A little later on he turned down one candidate for the course. She was an able woman doctor and the wife of another doctor. Both of them were staunch supporter and friends of Alexander's. The reason Alexander gave for rejecting her was that her co-ordination was too bad. As my own co-ordination and that of the young Scot who suffered from asthma were much worse than this doctor's, I could not believe in the validity of this reason, and the incident disturbed me.

But it was our unsupervised work in the afternoon that was most disturbing to me personally. I was a badly handicapped person, and this made me the favourite guinea pig among the students. Everyone liked to work on me because extraordinary things seemed to happen. Whatever was done to me produced very marked reactions and changes. Two colleagues in particular liked to work on me and what they often did was to take my head forward and down. This required no skill, and it caused all sorts of things to happen in the back. I sometimes thought at the end of the afternoon that my walking was more difficult, so I decided to 'manage' things. I saw to it that I worked with the more intelligent students in the afternoon, and whatever students I was with, if I did not like the way things were going, I protested. Because we worked in groups in the afternoon, it was easy to engineer things this way. I had my own flat in Chelsea, and I would invite the group I wanted to work with there.

Towards the end of that first year an incident occurred which involved all of us. Anthony Ludovici, a writer and pupil of Alexander's, was planning to write a book on Alexander's work to be called *Health and Education Through Self-Mastery*. He and Alexander were discussing the matter of putting in a chapter severely criticizing L. P. Jacks. Jacks was a lecturer, editor of the *Hibbert Journal*, and the head of Manchester College, Oxford; he was held in most affectionate esteem by his readers and his college. The grounds for criticism were that the speeches and articles of L. P. Jacks offered no technique for carrying out his ideas. Jacks was to be compared in this regard with Alexander, and unfavourably. We talked in class about Ludovci's book from time to time, and one day F. M. put it to us as a matter of class vote whether the chapter on L. P. Jacks should be included. F. M. was certainly not called on to consult his students about such a matter; yet, as he did so, we naturally believed that he was intending to give us a voice in the decision. We voted unanimously that the chapter should not be included. F. M. was very much annoyed and proceeded to tell Ludovici to include it. This disturbed some of us considerably. I felt it defined the part we would have in Alexander's plans and policies. It looked as if we might have no part unless we agreed with him completely.

His attitude towards us was very much like that of an uncle, but an uncle with no responsibility. As long as we caused him no trouble and did not cross him in any way, he liked to have us about. He liked us as an audience and as an inner circle which would always give him admiration and support. But when it came to a showdown, it was not likely that we would have any say whatsoever. As I thought about his attitude to us, his students, I began to speculate on his attitude to the rest of the world. Was '*der Tag*' really just around the corner? Certainly a number of good opportunities seemed to be 'on the boil' but it remained to be seen what would happen to them. Alexander had been teaching for many years; he must previously have had opportunities to further his work. What had happened to these? Was his attitude to us indicative of his outlook to the rest of the world?

He enjoyed companions and admirers, but was he capable of any relationship that required in the smallest degree a co-operative give and take?

Our outlook on Alexander underwent great changes during this first year. All of us, I think, had projected a hero-image on him. No human can support such an image for long. Fairly soon we were disillusioned. Then we thought of him as an ordinary human leader. He would feel responsible for teaching us, and we would co-operate to help further the work. Nothing could have been farther from the facts. He was neither an archetypal hero nor an ordinary man; he was a genius, going his own way with strength, impervious to the opinions of others thinking in a different way from most men, having different values as to what was important, attending to different things. As a natural sequence to this exaggeratedly individual outlook, it seemed as if it was literally impossible for him to see another person's point of view and more than impossible for him to give ear to it.

At this stage in the training course we began to grasp that fact, but still rather faintly. We knew the rules of the game were altered, but we did not quite know how or to what extent they would be altered. We began to suspect that we were to be on our own. We would have to hold *ourselves* responsible for learning his work as best we could. Alexander was there, and we might in some way learn how to get what we needed from him, or we might not. We could not count on him for anything. This was a hard thing to face, and at that time we did not fully face it. Rather we started worrying about it as a likely possibility.

The use of the word 'we' here is not strictly accurate. There was a small group of students who, in the face of heavy odds, clung to the image of an archetypal hero. They had their troubles, but I cannot say much about them as I am not sure what they went through. Only one colleague I know of felt by the time the course ended that he had been betrayed by F. M. Actually, he had built a false image of the man and had not looked at any facts or incidents that would have destroyed this image, so that the downfall when it came was great.

At the end of the first year, however, the students in the training course had fallen into two groups: one group felt the king could do no wrong; the other group felt that the king, being a genius, could and would do a great deal that was wrong from their point of view, but that what they were after was so valuable they were prepared to stay in the course whatever happened. There was no doubt about this on the part of anyone from either group. Parallel with my group's reappraisal of F. M. went our ever-increasing belief in the importance and value of his work and an acceptance of the fact that a genius simply could not be measured by the same yardstick as other men. The greatness of what he offered more than offset what he lacked.

I think if it had been suggested to him that he was somewhat irresponsible in regard to his training course because there were no initial qualifying requirements for his teachers and because ignorant beginners were allowed to work undirected on each other—he would at first have been hurt and puzzled. Later, of course, he would have been furious and felt persecuted, but the first reaction would have been hurt and genuine puzzlement. He had been prodded into starting a training course; well, he had started a training course; what else was there to it? And as to unsupervised work: these students had had vastly more help and guidance than he had ever had. Did people really have to be spoon-fed every half hour? I honestly think this is how he would have looked at it, and he would have envisaged no other problem. I had been looking at it from the point of view of what ordinarily took place in traditional educational circles. Only gradually did I realize that what took place in such circles had nothing to do with him. His mind did not concern itself with that type of problem. It is doubtful if he was even aware of what took place; his thinking was in another area. The great thing was that he had started a training course; we had a chance to learn his work. It was up to us to understand and fit in with him enough to be able to get what he had to offer.

It was necessary to remember that the very gifts and qualities which were assets to Alexander in making his discovery became liabilities when it came to establishing his work and training teachers. His 'lone wolf' quality, for example, helped him when he was working out his experiments, but handicapped him when he had to handle people. He had never handled people in groups nor had any experience in the kind of problems that groups presented. He was in no way fitted to do this kind of work. People and circumstances had edged him into this position. He had, perhaps unwittingly, allowed them to do so. At any rate, it was at times a very hard position for him.

Chapter 5

Our progress in learning
— some of the changes the work brought about in pupils

My group began the second year of the training course better equipped to meet whatever difficulties lay ahead of us. For the first time we were looking at Alexander and our professional situation realistically.

We knew that we would have to take the initiative in learning his work, and that since it was not likely F. M.' explanations would improve, our powers of observation seemed the best thing to rely on. He was, after all, 'showing' us rather than 'telling' us. So we began to observe carefully what F. M.'s hands were doing in a lesson and what changes occurred in a pupil; then as a group we discussed and appraised these observations. As a final step we would sometimes turn to F. M. for confirmation on doubtful points. The more we knew, the better chance we had of getting information from F. M.

Something else also helped us now. We had had a sufficient number of new experiences in our lessons for our intellectual belief in Alexander's principle to be changing into an actual belief. It was, for example, quite impossible for me, in the beginning, to *actually* believe that a foot was not best served by handling a foot. Although the HN & B pattern had revolutionized my walking and specific treatment of my feet and legs had produced negative results, this may seem almost incredible, but Herbert Spencer's remark that 'demonstration fails to alter established belief' is all too true. Bit by bit, however, as I continued to have new experiences, my old belief and orientation began to die, and the day came when I no longer wanted to have my feet touched. Now my actual belief was that nothing could help my feet and legs so much as having the HN & B pattern built up strongly and maintaining it while I used my legs.

Side by side with my now being experimentally rooted and

grounded in Alexander's principle, my intellectual grasp of it also became clearer and clearer. This was brought about by my reading the biologist G. E. Coghill's book, *Anatomy and the Problems of Behaviour*. In a pragmatic sense the findings of Coghill and Alexander are amazingly parallel, and as Coghill writes with exceptional clarity, his book threw added light on Alexander's work.

Through laboratory experiments on the amblystoma (or salamander) Coghill had discovered that there was a total pattern of integration in the animal, which proceeded from the head downward, and that there were also little partial patterns such as the movements of the fins and digits. In the beginning the fins and digits could not move unless the total pattern of integration initiated the movement; later, as the animal grows, the limbs gain some independence, but their functioning is never at its biological best unless the total pattern is maintained.

Alexander had found, in pragmatic experimentation upon himself and others, that there was a main body pattern which, when it was operating, brought about the best functioning of specific parts, such as arms, legs, jaw. But that when the specific parts became the 'boss' or leader and destroyed the main pattern, functioning was thrown out. And so Alexander's work is a continuous attempt to maintain this body pattern of the head, neck and back in all the body's activities, with the small partial patterns being subordinate to the main pattern.

A friend of mine, who had had great difficulty in understanding Alexander's work, after seeing the parallel between Alexander and Coghill, understood Alexander's principle for the first time. She said, 'I think of one main pattern and smaller partial patterns in terms of a tree growth that has a main trunk and diminishing-sized branches. The main trunk represents the main body pattern, which conditions and controls the diminishing-sized branches which represent the partial patterns. As opposed to a tree growth, I think of a bush growth which shoots equally important stems straight from the ground, and in which no one pattern is more important than any other pattern.' While no analogy is perfect, it can often give added life and understanding to something we had not clearly seen before. The HN & B pattern in combination with the partial patterns constitutes a total pattern of the organism. This is what F. M. meant when he said in my first interview: 'I am not interested in the particular manifestation of your wrongness.' He was concerned with a total pattern of the organism and not one symptom or four symptoms. As he once remarked to us in class, 'We are working on a principle whereby we tend to get rid of not *one* of our peculiarities but the *lot*.'

I remembered that my friend Catherine in her first series of lessons gained in tranquillity and lost her nervous craving for cigarettes. Mrs Brown's physical ailments were relieved, and she progressively lost her depression. A number of reactions of different sorts had altered after a change in the total pattern of the organism.

My concept of the work had changed, so that when someone outside would ask me: 'Were X's flat feet helped?' I'd say, 'Why, yes, of course, but actually that's not the most important thing that has happened to him. Can't you see some of the other differences yourself?'

When I noticed the changes that were taking place in some of the pupils at Ashley Place, it was always in terms of a total pattern. I remembered one dried-up, dead-looking little man who walked with two sticks. He never lifted his feet at all, just shuffled them along the floor. I would meet him sometimes in the hall at Ashley Place on his way to his lesson. For a long time I had not seen him and indeed had forgotten about him. Then one day I was on the street with a colleague just outside the entrance to Victoria Underground, and I saw him walking along with brisk, confident steps, no sticks in his hands, and a bright, alert look in his eyes. 'Good heavens,' I said to my colleague, 'isn't that the little man that comes to Ashley Place?' 'My word, it is!' she exclaimed. 'I remember F. M. said the other day that he had improved so much he only comes occasionally now.'

Another pupil, of about nine years of age, stands out in my

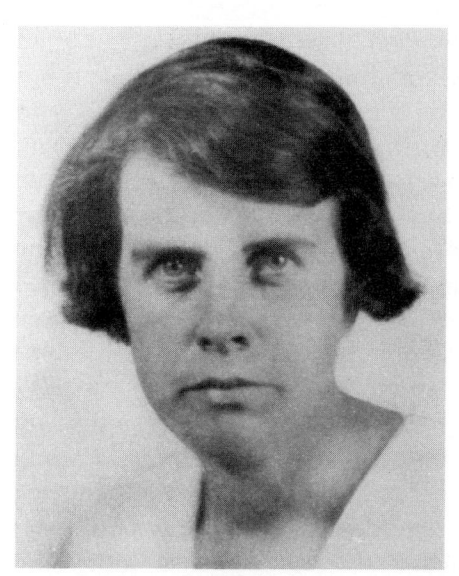

Fig. 6a. Passport photograph of the author taken June 1929, when she was going to England for her first two months' series of lessons with Alexander.

Fig. 6b. Passport photograph of the author taken August 1933, after she had had two years, seven months' work in the training course.

memory. I saw him first in the room used for the 'Little School' —a grey-faced, sad little boy. He was deaf and moved in a shambling way. His small face was grey and showed a quiet desperation. 'What a sweet little boy,' I thought, 'and yet (such was the sad and hopeless impression that he made on me) perhaps it would be better if he were to die.' The 'Little School' moved to Penhill shortly after that, and I did not see any of the children again until I went to Penhill for the usual end of term party almost a year later. The children were playing about, and one unusually attractive boy with sparkling eyes was boxing with another boy. I watched the match, and it slowly dawned on me that this was the same little boy for whom I had thought death would be a merciful release!

Such instances as these were everyday occurrences at 16 Ashley Place. We never got used to the wonder of them, and in addition to these transformations our enthusiasm was kept at a high pitch by the changes that were taking place in each one of us. Today Dr Wilfred Barlow, a practising physician and one of our teachers, has kept case histories of his pupils and has assembled a substantial body of medical evidence as to the changes that take place in pupils following a series of lessons.

While we had no such helpful records at the beginning of the second year of the training course, there were certain associated changes that took place in all students, though in varying degrees. These changes were visible and in many instances measurable.

The eyes of all the students were more alive and alert; their complexions were much better. The set of their heads on their necks was different, their necks being farther back and more in line with the dorsal spine. This set of the head was extremely pleasing aesthetically. Their heads also had an energized look of leading upwards. There was no sign of stiffness or strain attached to this; it was simply an appearance of energy upwards —the same arresting quality that one sees in the statue of the Winged Victory (Nike) of Samothrace (see fig. 7, p. 63).

The 'dowager's hump', that strategic place where there is a definite break between the neck and the dorsal spine and where the neck starts getting in front of the spine, was diminished in all members of the group; so were winged scapulae; shoulders were wider. The fit of the men's coats was very bad (it had become increasingly bad since the beginning of the course): their coats were too tight in the back and too loose in front. (This was because their backs had widened and their habit of initiating every movement by pressing out in front, 'frontal pressure', we called it, had lessened.) When the men took off their coats and you could see the fit of their vests, the change was even more apparent. The vests were strained tight over the back and inches too big in front—no fit at all. Most of them who had measured themselves in the beginning reported an increase in height.

The same type of changes occurred in the women as well, although they were not always so apparent because of the comparative looseness of women's clothes. Certain changes, however, took place that were peculiar to the women. One of the most aesthetically pleasing of these was a loss in the thickness of the torso from just below the breasts to the waist line. In some cases the breasts themselves became more fully developed and were carried higher. The contours of the women became more clear cut and more feminine. Both men and women acquired a more elongated appearance, even those who had gained in weight. The waistline dropped and decreased in size and the hip measurement decreased.

Such changes were common to all students, myself included. The changes in my own condition marked the high point in the course for me, but as important ones occurred right up to the end of the course, I prefer to summarize my own story at that time.

Incidentally, the student with asthma was not entirely free from it at that time, but the frequency and severity of his attacks had greatly lessened.

The general health of everyone in the course was excellent.

Fig. 7. Nike (Winged Victory) of Samothrace.

I also scrutinized my colleagues for changes of a less tangible nature. I believed that most of them thought in a more organized way, with less confusion and greater consciousness. Some handled their lives with more mastery and ease; they lived more successfully and happily. On the other hand, there were some who were not doing any better with their lives than they had been at the beginning of the course. That this last should be the case did not lessen the value of the work for me; rather it increased it.

The work was not a magic wand that was waved over you and changed you independently of your own efforts and outlook. It was something in which you must consciously choose to participate and make your own, if you expected great and lasting benefits.

A change that took place in all of us was that our sensory registration became more reliable. The reader must turn to Chapter 14 to read of Alexander's discovery of the unreliability of our feelings and how this temporarily thwarted his own progress. When he thought he was putting his head forward, for example, he was putting it back. When we think we are standing up straight, we are often twisting to one side. Whatever is familiar to us *feels* right; whatever is unfamiliar feels wrong. As the HN & B pattern gets more established, feeling becomes progressively more reliable, and because of this it is easier to improve. 'If we become sensorily aware of doing a harmful thing to ourselves, we can cease doing it.'*

It is difficult to account for these and all the other changes that are mentioned in this book in terms of current physiological thinking. Nevertheless, they are therapeutically significant, and Alexander's new HN & B pattern, although it is a radical departure from what medicine knows and uses, can be explored experimentally.

---

* Alexander in conversation with the author.

Chapter 6

Alexander and Opportunities

The story of the training course had become for me that of two connecting dramas. My personal drama as a student was: could I learn enough from Alexander to become a competent teacher? The larger drama was whether in the long run Alexander was going to promote or halt his own work. I had seen how his inadequate explanations impeded his work, and now I was to see him kill what seemed to be a particularly constructive opportunity offered him by a pupil and supporter of long standing. Although we had reason to know by this time that opportunities for spreading the work had a mysterious way of dying, when F. M. told us one day in 1933 that Miss Esther Lawrence, one-time head of the Froebel Institute but now retired, had bought a house on Cromwell Road to be used for an Alexander School for Children, we were naïvely filled with hope.

For a number of years Alexander had had a school for a small group of children who were taught the Alexander Technique and how to apply it to their school work and activities, but as the school did not meet the ordinary academic requirements, the children came for rather short periods, most of them were handicapped, and the number in the school was always small.

Alexander had always spoken as if a school for children run on his principles but meeting the ordinary educational requirements was the dream of his heart. His enthusiastic followers also felt that this would be one of the most worthwhile developments that could take place in the work. It now looked as if this dream would come true.

Miss Lawrence planned to bring back some of her best old Froebel teachers to teach the academic subjects. F. M. was to be the final authority, with unlimited power. We of the training course were to teach the Alexander work to the children and help them apply it in their studies and school activities. This was welcome news indeed, both because it would promote the work in a new and important way, and because it would give us some much needed teaching practice. We had had no practice teaching, and no prospect of any. The sherry glasses came out (as usual) and we all drank sherry in honour of the occasion.

The appearance of the sherry glasses might have warned us that a familiar pattern had begun again, but somehow it didn't. Buying a house was such a tangible thing, and as the house was actually there on Cromwell Road and was now owned by Miss Lawrence, it seemed well nigh impossible to believe that it would not be used for a school. What indeed could prevent its being used for one? Miss Lawrence bought some furniture and installed a housekeeper. One member of the training course boarded there. I remember going through the house for the first time and how happy we all felt. We looked at the room in the house which was to be F. M.'s 'office'—a nice, roomy place—here he was to have the chance to carry out his ideas and principles (Miss Lawrence always stressed this) and every possible help would be given him. As for us, we felt we were going to get just the kind of practice teaching we so needed and wanted.

In the house was a large-size room or hall with a platform at one end of it, and fairly soon after the purchase of the house we started using this room for our rehearsals of *The Merchant of Venice,* which we expected to act before an astonished London at some time in the near future. So we began to use the house in this way, but sadly enough we never used it in any other way. Almost at once the usual veils of obscurity began to drop over the school idea. In fact, I never heard F. M. mention the word 'school' after we drank sherry together.

That summer, for my August holiday I went to an Italian villa belonging to the father of a colleague. She had asked another colleague out for the last part of the month. When he arrived, he told us that he and another student had seen F. M. recently and that F. M. had said he thought perhaps it was *not exactly the right time to start a school now*. This was the only direct information we ever had about F. M.'s change of mind in regard to the school project.

It was not spoken of when we returned to London in September, and we continued to use the house until after our play was produced. Nor had we any direct information as to the final showdown—which must have occurred—with Miss Lawrence. Miss Lawrence, when seen, looked somewhat shattered. She sold the house soon afterwards. So ended both the story of Miss Lawrence's school and our hopes of receiving a more adequate training through this school.

It was deeply disheartening for us to have such an opportunity as Miss Lawrence's school destroyed. Most of us now thought that '*der Tag*' was probably not going to take place at all—at least not in our lifetimes. But we continued to believe that if we could just manage to become good teachers our training would be most rewarding and most worthwhile, so strong was our belief in the importance of Alexander's work and our enthusiasm for it.

There was no mention in our class as to why the school project was abandoned. One could only conjecture what had actually gone on in F. M.'s mind at that time. It seemed to me it must have been something like this: an opportunity presented itself, and he welcomed it as it increased his prestige and importance. Then gradually he commenced to sense where it would lead. It would lead to the necessity for cooperation and give-and-take with other people; other people might even criticize him; he might be forced to adopt some of their ways; he would no longer be monarch of all he surveyed, no longer accountable to no one. As this picture took shape in his mind, F. M. must have felt that the opportunity would have to be killed.

Some years later when Sir Stafford Cripps was trying to found an Alexander Teachers' Society and read to F. M. the plan of organization, a colleague told me that F. M. exclaimed, 'Why, under this scheme I could be outvoted!' and refused to give it his support. Perhaps this is the story in F. M.'s own words. No matter how attractive opportunities seemed to him in the beginning or how enhancing to his prestige, in the end they boiled down to this one bleak fact: he could be outvoted. Certainly he wanted to keep the work entirely in his own hands, and while I believe that one important reason for this was his constitutional inability to participate in a co-operative enterprise, there was also the more legitimate reason that he wished to protect and preserve his work. He knew how prone the public and even some of his own followers were to distort his work, water it down so that it would be more in line with the popular taste, destroy its uniqueness and in so doing destroy the work itself. But whatever his reasons were, he had an indiscriminate and blanket way of killing the opportunities offered to him.

As the course continued, we were to see still another way in which Alexander with, I believe, complete unawareness held back the acceptance of his work.

Distrust was aroused by the way he spoke and wrote. Many were the broad generalizations and startling statements to which he gave utterance. I remember one morning his coming briskly into our classroom, looking very pleased with himself, and saying, 'Belief is a matter of customary muscle tension.'

'F. M.,' I said, 'don't you mean that belief about what you can do with the body is a matter of customary muscle tension?' The discussion was on. He kept talking while he worked. Finally at the end of the morning's work F. M. said, 'Yes, belief about what you can do with the body is a matter of customary muscle tension.'

My colleagues thought I was stupid to try to pin him down. What did it matter? We knew what he meant and I would just annoy him.

'Besides, maybe there is something in what he says,' one colleague remarked. 'People often change their outlooks around here as they get on in the work.'

'Yes, that's true,' I said, 'but the point is that he cannot substantiate the statement that "belief is a matter of customary muscle tension." It's the reliability of his statements that I am fussing about. I think that is important. If he talks like this to us, he will do so to other people and their trust in his work will be shaken.'

Indeed, that very afternoon when we went to visit his little school for children, which was now at Penhill, Sidcup, I heard F. M. saying to one of the mothers, 'Belief is a matter of customary muscle tension.' The woman looked bewildered and suspicious.

Most of all F. M. enjoyed making statements that were calculated to startle. I remember one morning when, after looking around the class rather tentatively as if to see how we would take it, F. M. declared: 'The trouble with Christ was that his technique was weak.' Having made this pronouncement, he looked very pleased with himself.

I believe that often when he made startling statements he was simply putting himself in the role of an actor who wished to electrify his audience. There was always his small band of worshippers who received his statements with awestruck admiration. In the majority of people, however, his words aroused antagonism and distrust.

It was the way in which he wrote and spoke about the term Primary Control that perhaps did the greatest damage to his work. He implied and sometimes said outright that he had discovered a Primary Control in the sense of a physiological entity and that it was identical with the Central Control discovered by Rudolf Magnus.

I quote here a statement made by Alexander in his book, *The Use of the Self*, page 60.

> ... *this primary control* called by the late Prof. Magnus, of Utrecht, the Central Control ...

Alexander was dealing with a concept which belonged in the fields of science and medicine—he was therefore judged as a scientist, not as a layman. Everyone knew that a physiological entity could not be discovered by the method of experimentation that Alexander used. He was claiming something to be so when it had not been proved that it was so. If he had said, 'I have discovered a head, neck and back pattern that *acts* as if it were a Primary Control,' his position would have been impregnable.

The same thing was true when he identified his 'Primary

Control' with the Central Control discovered by Magnus. Rudolf Magnus, a noted physiologist, through his laboratory work on animals had discovered that the head led and determined the attitudinal reflexes of the rest of the body. There is a strong analogy between his discovery and that of Alexander's, and it is a possible hypothesis that Magnus and Alexander discovered the same thing, but this hypothesis has never been proven and so it could not be stated as an accepted fact.

The task of getting a new concept accepted in science and medicine is difficult under the best of circumstances. The element of newness alone makes it suspect. But if in addition the originator of the concept makes statements about it which cannot be fully substantiated, the acceptance of his work is held back.

Alexander's nickname, when he visited the United States during the First World War, was 'the confidence man who really did have the gold brick.' This is interesting: the first impression he gave out was that of a 'confidence man', but once his work was known and experienced, people readily acknowledged that he 'really did have the gold brick'.

Alexander was not aware that he had harmed his work by what he said, and he would not have understood how he had done so. To him, knowledge was something that worked—it solved the problem. He would speak with bewilderment of heart specialists dying of heart disease, of oculists going blind. 'What use is their knowledge?' he would ask. While he would sometimes reluctantly admit that it might be of value in surgery, nevertheless such a concept of knowledge cut into and contradicted his own belief. The Primary Control had 'worked' for close on to sixty years and on several thousand people. To Alexander's mind it was no longer a hypothesis but a proven fact. With this outlook he would not consider that he was making a false statement about it when he implied that it was a physiological entity. It worked, it was real, it must therefore exist in a concrete, tangible way.

Chapter 7

THE MERCHANT OF VENICE

In our third year there began one of the strangest and most bizarre stories of our entire course. We met head on, as it were, F. M.'s pent-up frustrations and ambitions in regard to acting and the theatre. Certainly at this time acting claimed his first allegiance and was more important to him than his own work and our professional training. A great many assumptions that I had clung to about Alexander, his interest in training teachers, in having a school for children, in establishing his work, at this time faded.

The story started quietly enough by F. M. coming into the class one morning and saying that he thought we would put on *The Merchant of Venice* at the Old Vic and Sadler's Wells. This did sound a little startling, for only one in the group was a professional actor, and except for two of us we were all quite deplorable even as amateur actors. And although I had always known that F. M. had a fervent interest in acting, I could not see that this gave his startling and time-consuming project any legitimate place in his training course for teachers.

I had a vain hope that because of the expense such a project would prove impractical, but no! F. M. had arranged that the Alexander Trust Fund was to advance the money, and this was to be repaid by the revenue from the sale of tickets.

The first viewpoint voiced by F. M. was that there was no particular reason for us to make this public appearance because of our acting ability. This was all too true. He said he considered it important, however, that we appear on the public stage to show how we handled ourselves from the point of view of both voice and movement. The public would know that we had not been trained in any specific way but that we would simply be illustrating what his technique would do for movements and voice production on the stage.

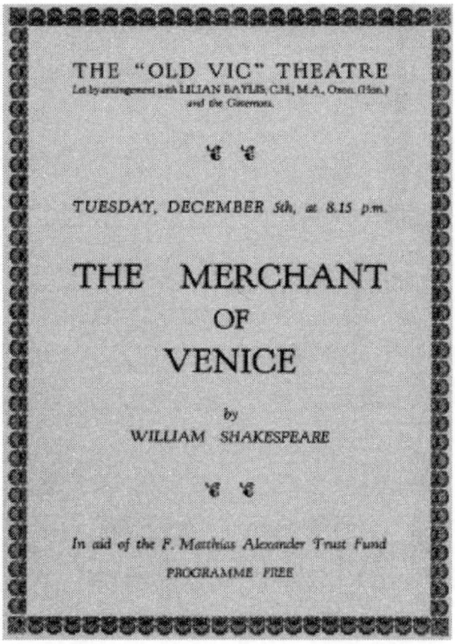

THE "OLD VIC" THEATRE
Let by arrangement with LILIAN BAYLIS, C.H., M.A., Oxon. (Hon.) and the Governors.

TUESDAY, DECEMBER 5th, at 8.15 p.m.

THE MERCHANT OF VENICE

by WILLIAM SHAKESPEARE

In aid of the F. Matthias Alexander Trust Fund

PROGRAMME FREE

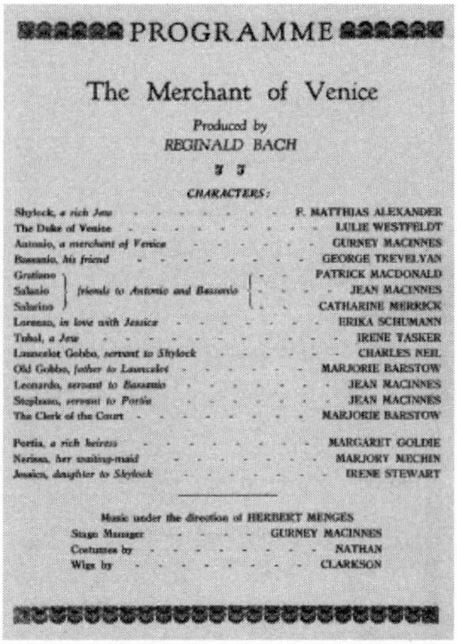

PROGRAMME

The Merchant of Venice

Produced by REGINALD BACH

CHARACTERS:

Shylock, a rich Jew	F. MATTHIAS ALEXANDER
The Duke of Venice	LULIE WESTFELDT
Antonio, a merchant of Venice	GURNEY MACINNES
Bassanio, his friend	GEORGE TREVELYAN
Gratiano (friends to Antonio and Bassanio)	PATRICK MACDONALD
Salanio (friends to Antonio and Bassanio)	JEAN MACINNES
Salarino (friends to Antonio and Bassanio)	CATHARINE MERRICK
Lorenzo, in love with Jessica	ERIKA SCHUMANN
Tubal, a Jew	IRENE TASKER
Launcelot Gobbo, servant to Shylock	CHARLES NEIL
Old Gobbo, father to Launcelot	MARJORIE BARSTOW
Leonardo, servant to Bassanio	JEAN MACINNES
Stephano, servant to Portia	JEAN MACINNES
The Clerk of the Court	MARJORIE BARSTOW
Portia, a rich heiress	MARGARET GOLDIE
Nerissa, her waiting-maid	MARJORY MECHIN
Jessica, daughter to Shylock	IRENE STEWART

Music under the direction of HERBERT MENGES

Stage Manager	GURNEY MACINNES
Costumes by	NATHAN
Wigs by	CLARKSON

Fig. 8. Programme for *The Merchant of Venice*, 1933, p. 1 and 2.

There was some sanity in this point of view; slight, perhaps, but at least some.

Alexander's work has frequently been linked with acting. His first work when he came to London from Australia was in the theatre. Throughout the course there was generally some actor or actress coming to Ashley Place for lessons because of the help it gave them in their profession. So at first it did not seem too unreasonable that we, as amateurs, should put on a play as a means of illustrating what his work could do for voice production and movement. But as time went on all sanity seemed to leave everything. F. M. trained us himself—he trained us assiduously for months. We got worse and worse. In addition to everything else we became stale. For a long time F. M. seemed to be so full of delight at acting again (he was Shylock, of course) and producing a play, that he had no room for any other thought or feeling. He simply had no notion of how awful we were.

He took hours off from his private teaching for rehearsals, which must have cut down his income drastically. Our morning classes went on as usual except that all conversation and interest were directed towards the play; but our afternoon work, in which we were embarking on the struggle of learning to use our hands on each other, was drastically curtailed.

Psychologically the way things were going affected some of us quite unhappily. We had staked a great deal to get this training, and it was becoming increasingly doubtful if we were going to get what we needed as teachers. The enormous amount of time devoted to the play was hard to tolerate. It was at this time that the phrase 'Ashley Place Blues' was first coined. It was used to describe any student who seemed anxious and unhappy.

Finally one day, after long months of directing us himself, F. M. appeared with a producer, Reginald Bach. It had evidently become clear even to F. M. that dramatically speaking, things were in a very bad way. Bach was a nice man and a good producer, but of course the fact that we were now to be whipped into shape by a professional director annihilated the intention that F. M. had originally expressed in regard to the play, i.e. that we were not to demonstrate any sort of dramatic training but were to illustrate to the public only what Alexander's technique would do for bodily movements and for voice production on the stage. After rehearsals sometimes a small group of us would go to a pub for beer, and Bach would occasionally accompany us. He said when he first saw and heard us he thought that we were the most hopeless group he had ever encountered. Then, the thing that greatly impressed him was that we seemed to have an ability, in spite of wrong training and over-training, to lift ourselves out of the morass into which we had fallen and to follow his directions. He considered this so unusual that he wanted to arrange with F. M. to have some lessons to see what it was that gave us this rare ability to change our habit pattern and right ourselves.

In the training course there were different and conflicting attitudes towards the play. A small group had become stage struck; even those who couldn't act (and there were only two who could) were infected with this fever. Some of them thought it was nonsense, but fun, notwithstanding. A third group, to

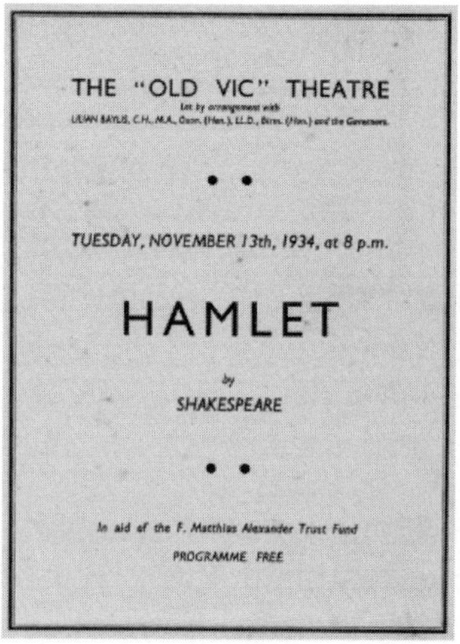
THE "OLD VIC" THEATRE
Let by arrangement with
LILIAN BAYLIS, C.H., M.A., Oxon. (Hon.), LL.D., Birm. (Hon.) and the Governors.

TUESDAY, NOVEMBER 13th, 1934, at 8 p.m.

HAMLET
by
SHAKESPEARE

In aid of the F. Matthias Alexander Trust Fund
PROGRAMME FREE

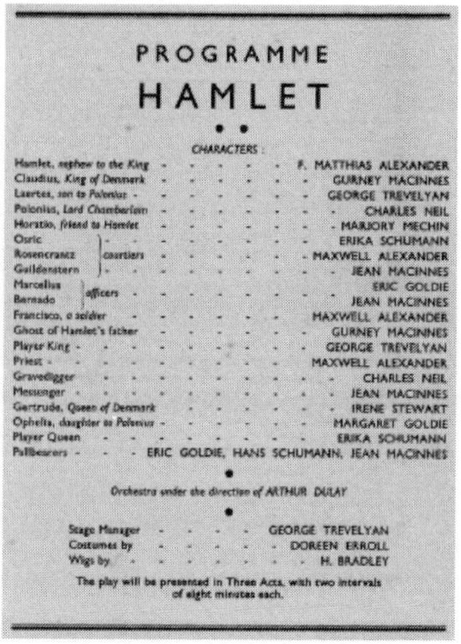
PROGRAMME
HAMLET

CHARACTERS:

Hamlet, *nephew to the King*	F. MATTHIAS ALEXANDER
Claudius, *King of Denmark*	GURNEY MACINNES
Laertes, *son to Polonius*	GEORGE TREVELYAN
Polonius, *Lord Chamberlain*	CHARLES NEIL
Horatio, *friend to Hamlet*	MARJORY MECHIN
Osric (courtiers)	ERIKA SCHUMANN
Rosencrantz (courtiers)	MAXWELL ALEXANDER
Guildenstern (courtiers)	JEAN MACINNES
Marcellus (officers)	ERIC GOLDIE
Bernado (officers)	JEAN MACINNES
Francisco, *a soldier*	MAXWELL ALEXANDER
Ghost of Hamlet's father	GURNEY MACINNES
Player King	GEORGE TREVELYAN
Priest	MAXWELL ALEXANDER
Gravedigger	CHARLES NEIL
Messenger	JEAN MACINNES
Gertrude, *Queen of Denmark*	IRENE STEWART
Ophelia, *daughter to Polonius*	MARGARET GOLDIE
Player Queen	ERIKA SCHUMANN
Pallbearers	ERIC GOLDIE, HANS SCHUMANN, JEAN MACINNES

Orchestra under the direction of ARTHUR DULAY

Stage Manager	GEORGE TREVELYAN
Costumes by	DOREEN ERROLL
Wigs by	H. BRADLEY

The play will be presented in Three Acts, with two intervals of eight minutes each.

Fig. 9. Programme for *Hamlet*, 1934, p. 1 and p. 3.

which I belonged, was genuinely distressed. We felt it was a serious misuse of our time, that we were getting farther and farther away from necessary training required by our profession, and that F. M.'s mounting frenzy was alarming. I remember Bach's remark about F. M. at this time; he likened him to a man who had something explosive in his system and he had to get rid of it.

F. M. had decided that I was to be Launcelot Gobbo. To me this was the last straw. I thought the public production of the play ridiculous and was harassed and disheartened because of all the time, interest and energy that was being put into it. I believed unhappily enough that F. M. would never remotely give to our training what he gave to the play, but if the play had not been there to consume him, he would at least have granted us more of his time and interest. I dismally asked a colleague why F. M. had picked me for Gobbo. She said he thought I was a wit. Whatever idea he had about this, he was progressively disillusioned. A more drearily static Gobbo never stood up before an audience. I was not trying to be unpleasant about it; it was simply not possible, without acting ability and feeling as I did inside, to caper about in a witty, lively way and perform the difficult part of Launcelot Gobbo.

> ## FOREWORD
>
> IN thanking all those who have given us their support in this venture, we should like to take the opportunity of explaining our reasons for producing this play. As many of our audience will know, this is the second dramatic production given by Mr. F. M. Alexander and the students of his Training Course. Last year we gave two performances of "The Merchant of Venice" at Sadlers Wells and the Old Vic in aid of the F. Matthias Alexander Trust Fund, to which the proceeds of the present performance will also be given.
>
> Mr. Alexander's work is not concerned with the theatre as such, nor, indeed, with any one activity. In his Training Course, he is endeavouring to teach his students how to improve the way in which they use themselves in the performance of every act of daily life, and his technique is based on the discoveries described in his last book, "The Use of the Self." Through this training, the student gradually develops a greater awareness and control of what he is doing with himself and this knowledge is of value to him in any activity, particularly when this involves new and therefore unfamiliar experiences. Apart from the work done for last year's performances, none of the students have had any theatrical experience or training, nor do any of them intend to take up the theatre as a career. Mr. Alexander, who is now 65, himself abandoned his career as a reciter over thirty years ago, in order to devote himself entirely to the teaching of his technique. Since the production of a play involves a wide range of activities demanding control of speech, movement, gesture and expression, it gives the students a particularly interesting opportunity of attempting to apply, under difficult and comparatively unfamiliar conditions, the same principles which they are learning to put into practice in everyday life.
>
> The members of the cast wish to acknowledge their great indebtedness to Mr. Reginald Bach for his valuable help and advice in the preparation of the play.
>
> Further information about the Trust Fund and the Training Course will be found on the last page of this programme.

Fig. 10. Programme for *Hamlet*, 1934, p. 2.

F. M. really laboured with me. He was untiring. In teaching me this role of Gobbo he was more of a *teacher* than I have ever seen him. He still 'showed' me rather than used words to tell me about it, but in this instance showing me was the right thing to do, and he did it to perfection. He himself would have made a superb Gobbo. Even in his use of words I have never heard him more fluent or to the point, and, wonder of wonders, he actually seemed to try to get in touch with my mind in an attempt to remove whatever impediments were deadening me. Finally, however, F. M. gave up. He decided that he had made a mistake in casting me as Gobbo, and he said I could be the Doge of Venice instead. I was delighted—in so far as anything about this play could delight me. The Doge was a less conspicuous, less exacting part and it did not require abilities that were utterly beyond my powers at this time, and indeed at any time. It was unfortunate, perhaps, that the Doge of Venice should be a woman, and a woman with an American accent, but so many unfortunate things of greater magnitude were taking place that this did not really seem to matter.

After it was decided that I was to be the Doge, F. M. came and told me that he, personally, would put my beard on for me! It was a mark of high favour. Apparently he wished to make me happy, or even to placate me! I was at a loss to know what to think. We appeared to be in topsy-turvy land. Where was the man who had asked us to vote on whether or not Ludovici should include the chapter on L. P. Jacks in his book, and who, when we voted 'No', was much annoyed and advised Ludovici to put it in anyway? Then, our co-operation had not mattered to him. Now it did. He had consideration for all of us now. He wanted, so far as it was possible, to keep us happy and to work *with* us.

Plans were under way to produce *Hamlet* the following year. The original purpose of the training course seemed to have been lost sight of completely. Training courses were to go on and on producing plays. I remember several members of the training course mentioning at this time that it seemed just possible that the training course was started so F. M. would have a troupe of actors at his disposal. In one way the idea appeared incredible; in another, it appeared to be the only hypothesis that made intelligible what was happening.

F. M. literally had the strength of ten. Nothing was too much for him, no sacrifice of time or money, no struggle or effort was too great. Inevitably, we thought back to the time when he had been discovering the HN & B pattern, the tremendous, lonely effort of nine years, in the face of what had seemed to be overwhelming odds. People had asked us sometimes what it was that had made him keep on, and we ourselves had wondered what emotional drive could have been strong enough to carry him through those appalling, difficult years. We were now seeing a drive stronger than anything we had yet encountered in him—stronger indeed than anything we could have envisaged.

I remember F. M. remarking the day before the play that a friend had just said to him, 'Tomorrow you will be the proudest man in London.' The only thing one could be sure of was that the source of his pride would not be in our manner of moving on the stage, or in our voice production, but in acting—his own acting—and possibly a little of ours in combination with his. His original viewpoint, if his words had ever really expressed his original viewpoint, had disappeared.

The night of the play I was sitting in the audience during the first part, as the Doge does not come on to the stage until towards the end. Before the curtain rose, something happened which gave us all immense pleasure. After the lights in the house had gone down, F. M. came out in front of the curtain to make a few introductory remarks, but for several minutes no remarks were possible. At the sight of him the audience broke into a spontaneous roar of applause. It was their tribute to the man and his work. His students and admirers had always felt that some such public tribute was long overdue, and this ovation was wonderful to hear, and it was wonderful to get back for even a few moments to the greatness of F. M.'s own work.

I do not believe that F. M. had any idea that he was receiving one of the great personal ovations of his life. He was linking it up with the play (not a line of which had yet been spoken) and he was wholly immersed in thoughts of the production.

It is difficult to give an account of the play because, of course, it sagged pretty badly. We had attempted something that required the finest acting, and—well, that was

78   F. Matthias Alexander: The Man and his Work

Fig. 11. Charles Neil, Gurney MacInnes and Irene Stewart in *Hamlet*.

Fig. 12. Gurney MacInnes, [unidentified] and George Trevelyan in *Hamlet*.

Fig. 13. Students in *Hamlet*, 1934.

unfortunate. Still, there was the glamour and the footlights, fine costumes, and beautiful lines. And now and then we would get a bit of acting. Launcelot Gobbo was first-rate and held the house. Portia was both moving and convincing. Unfortunately F. M. as Shylock was neither moving nor convincing. He simply did not ring true, though technically he was excellent in the role of Shylock. Anything that Bach had pointed out in the way of stage business, gesture and intonation he had picked up at once and he carried out Bach's instructions perfectly. But, to put it succinctly, he did not have the talent required for such a role and there was nothing that could make up for this lack of talent.

In view of the fact that the public had been told not to expect anything in the way of acting, I suppose we were probably adequate enough. I remember reading a review the next day in a paper—I think it was the *Daily Telegraph*—which went something like this: F. Matthias Alexander and a group of his students had put on *The Merchant of Venice* at the Old Vic. They did not, however, expect to be judged on their acting ability, and this being the case, the reviewer had no comment to make.

A number of people from the audience, however, gave us very favourable comments on the way we had handled ourselves on the stage. The consensus of opinion seemed to be that we did not have the usual amateurish look as we moved about. And that, at least, was heartening. After the play we went to Miss Lawrence's house in Cromwell Road and had a terrific party, no expense spared.

Shortly after this we put on the play again at Sadler's Wells, but there is nothing new to relate about this second performance. It went off much as the first one had. One could not see what had been accomplished by either performance that would justify the training course in continuing its dramatic activities, but F. M. was fully determined to put on *Hamlet* the following year. This, however, would not affect me personally, as by that time I would have finished the course and have returned to the United States.

It would be difficult for anyone who has not had this day-to-day association with F. M. throughout the period of his dramatic activities to fully understand the man or his motivation. To see him put on a play is to be given a basic clue to his character.

Chapter 8

Learning to be teachers

While these events were happening in the course, we were also struggling along somewhat unsuccessfully with our own personal problems as students. Were we going to learn enough from Alexander to become skilled teachers?

We had had a difficult time learning Alexander's work as pupils, but now, when we had to learn as teachers to use our hands on others, our task was a much harder one. Indeed, it now seems a miracle that we succeeded at all.

The first essential for a teacher is to be able to get the HN & B pattern functioning in a pupil. This pattern consists of a number of steps in a sequence. The second one, 'head *forward* in relation to the neck', is overwhelmingly difficult and has caused the failure of more teachers than any other factor or combination of factors.

F. M.'s method of teaching us how to get this step was first to have us put our hands on a fellow student's head; then he would place his hands on top of ours; and with a quick movement he would take the student's head 'forward in relation to the neck'.

This did not enable us to do it ourselves, as the mind and body do not work thus separately and apart from each other. Before the teacher can do the right thing with his hands, his mind must envisage the whole problem.

The problem of taking the head forward in relation to the neck involves several interdependent objectives. There must, for example, be a balanced relationship between the head and neck: the head tending to go forward as the neck tends to go back, the jaw must tend to go freely out, not down and not contracting into itself, as this will prevent the head from going up; the head must also be taken forward in such a manner that the symmetry and alignment of the body will not be affected unfavourably, and if possible they should be affected favourably; and finally, as the head of each pupil is placed differently on his neck, there must be variation in what the hands of the teacher must do in every case.

This most difficult step of 'head forward' requires lucid, detailed explanation as well as manual demonstration if the student is to acquire the understanding and manual skill necessary to bring it about.

We were getting no such help. We were simply floundering; our knowledge consisted of bits and pieces; there was no unifying element bringing all these separate elements into an intelligible whole. An appalling amount of time was wasted, and as the months passed our confusion deepened and our anxiety mounted. F. M. expressed no criticism of our performance and this confused us, as we did not know if he was satisfied about it or just not interested. To me he appeared somewhat abstracted about it, and I felt his attitude to be, 'Well, "you can lead a horse to water but you can't make him drink." I'll show them the right thing; maybe they will get it; maybe they won't.' Certainly he evinced no concern as to whether we got it or not.

I remember thinking one day that almost any intelligent person could do with his hands what I was doing, if he would give his attention to the matter for about six weeks. Surely, I thought, there must be more to Alexander's work than this. The colleagues we worked on sometimes felt 'light' as they stood up or walked about, but, as we rightly surmised, this was simply the result of an undue lengthening which required no skill and was a far cry indeed from the balanced lengthening and widening of the HN & B pattern which resulted in the body operating on a new control. Fortunately some of us had sense enough to know that we were producing no such basic change in the body of any colleague we worked on.

And then, when things looked darkest, help came!

We were saved by two unexpected happenings. The first was that we were given an extra year! One rainy afternoon in our third year we were in Miss Lawrence's house on Cromwell Road trying out for the different parts in *The Merchant of Venice*. At the end of our tryouts when we were about to get our coats and hats, a colleague came into the room with a message from F. M. (he had already left the room) saying he would keep us on for an extra year. Some of us were so relieved that we thought nothing, at the time, about the manner in which we were told this extremely important news or the attendant circumstances. We knew that if we had left at the end of our third year we could not possibly have survived as teachers.

While relief was my first reaction, I soon found myself suspecting that this gift of a fourth year might have something to do with *The Merchant of Venice*. Although new members had entered the training course, F. M. would have found it difficult to have put on a Shakespearean play without the original eight members. We would have left at the end of our third year, and the play took place in our fourth year. My suspicions were somewhat strengthened by subsequent events. There was never any talk with F. M. about this fourth year, no discussion of why we knew so little or what we could do to improve our work. In our professional training until the play was over we had less of his time and effort, not more. But it was so wonderful to have this extra time that it well nigh reconciled me to *The Merchant of Venice*.

Some of us found it hard to manage this fourth year, for even without an additional fee there was still the matter of living expenses, but we all did stay. F. M.'s work had become so important to us and we had made such Herculean efforts to get it, we could not face missing this final chance.

We had more time, but we also needed something more than time. We were confused, and because of our confusion we were inarticulate. We felt that we had not gotten what we expected or needed from the training course.

Finally, one day when all of my group were together, the second unexpected thing happened. One of my colleagues came out and expressed our problems in words, clearly and forcefully. He said in effect, 'We have missed the boat. We really do not know what the Primary Control is. We cannot get it at will with our hands. We have got to realize this as we work, and somehow or other pull ourselves up by our own bootstraps until we have some solid ground under our feet.' It was a great relief to hear him say this. We had known it in a way, but not with sufficient clarity to be able to express it. Without his clear sensing of the problem and his creative thought in helping us solve it, we would have failed as teachers, fourth year or no fourth year. This colleague, by clearing up a basic point, had resolved our confusion and doubt. This made the greatest difference to us, and our work together became increasingly rewarding. We worked as in a laboratory, using each other as guinea pigs, the group mind gradually bringing to light the problems involved in getting the HN & B pattern to function. Simultaneously our minds and our hands advanced in knowledge. As I look back upon this time it seems to me that the colleague who expressed our problem was the leading mind in getting us out of the swamp. In time we became knowledgeable enough to pick F. M.'s brains, and this gave us confirmation of what we had found out and insights into further knowledge. So we learned, as one doctor put it, 'to handle the controls.' Just as the driver of an automobile does not handle the individual parts of the engine but the controls of the car, so the Alexander teacher does not handle individual muscles but the HN & B pattern, which experimentally had been found to act as if it were a main control.

So in the fourth year of the training course my group learned what to do as teachers, but our next task was to build up skill in doing it. The mastery of any such art has this two-fold aspect: the knowledge of what should be done and the acquiring of skill in doing it.

In learning to use our hands on a pupil both time and grinding discipline were required, for we had to have our own HN & B pattern going as we put our hands on another pupil. The student teacher must be conscious that his HN & B pattern is leading and that his hands and arms (partial patterns) are subordinate to this main pattern.

So much time had been wasted in the training course, and our objective was such a hard one, that to get the skill we needed we saw that we would have to put more time, more work, and more money into our training than we had ever imagined. So while we had solid ground under our feet when the training course ended, my group planned to continue working together whenever possible. I hoped to return in summers and work with them. The training we needed was analogous in some degree to that required in mastering a skill or art. Training of this sort takes time, it cannot be achieved by verbal information. Words can make it easier to get an experience by doing away with intellectual barriers, but they are never the equivalent of the experience itself.

Whatever troubles we went through and whatever developments came afterwards, my group emerged from their training skilled teachers to the last man. And we are all working as teachers today.

The factors making our success possible were the realistic appraisal of F. M., belief in and enthusiasm for his work, creative resourcefulness, ability to stand prolonged discipline, and ability to work together as a group with trust and cooperation.

Chapter 9

A PERSONAL EXPERIENCE

The high point in the training course for me was the change in my own individual condition. My main reason for entering the course had been to get help for myself, and my hopes had not been disappointed. As the course neared its end, Bunyan's words from *Pilgrim's Progress* came into my mind: 'though with great difficulty I have got hither, yet now I do not repent me of all the trouble I have been at to arrive where I am.'

The changes that took place with me during my first two months of lessons I have already written of in some detail. In brief, they were greater ease and endurance in standing and walking, a straighter, longer back (my height increased one inch in those two months), lower, wider shoulders, no more hunching up of the left shoulder with every movement, my whole frame coming into a more normal alignment, muscular development of my calves (particularly the right calf), a different alignment of my arms in their sockets.

Then came the changes that I shared with the other members of the course during our first year of training.

At the beginning of the second year I had an individual change that marked a mountain peak for me.

It is strange how, in an unhappy or happy experience, one remembers vividly the details of one's surroundings and little, unimportant happenings. Thus when awareness came to me after my first operation that I would never again be able to run or to walk fast, or climb hills and stairs with the ease that I used to have before the operation, I remember vividly the details of the honeysuckle thicket where I was sitting. Now, at the end of the first year of the training course when a different type of experience came to me, I remember a cold spring morning in my rooms on Cromwell Road. My breakfast tray had just come up, and I was in my dressing gown and bedroom slippers, walking across the room to the table where the tray had been placed. Suddenly I felt a very strange sensation, not pleasant or unpleasant, but overwhelmingly strange. For a moment I did not know what had happened. Then I realized that my right heel was touching the floor. It was no longer up in the air but flat on the floor like the left one. It had not touched the floor for upwards of twenty years; shortly after the operation that had immobilized the right ankle, my right heel had drawn up and been unable to touch the floor. The sensation became more and more delightful. Almost at once, my balance became much more secure.

My improved balance made it possible for me to wear low shoes. After the operation when the surgeon realigned the right foot (the one with the fixed ankle), he said he did not see why I could not wear low shoes even though my heel was drawn up. His physiotherapist said the same. But when I tried it out, my ankle was still just as wobbly and insecure as it had ever been.

It is significant that both the surgeon and the physiotherapist had considered only the foot and ankle. They had handled them and looked at them and said this was all right and that was all right. But at no time had they included in their calculations how the functioning of the rest of the body might affect the foot and ankle. Something more than the foot operation was needed to give me a secure balance, and this something more, after twenty years, I now had.

Wearing low shoes started off a series of happenings that added up to what might be called a small psychological revolution. My clothes had never looked right with high boots, and so I had no interest in them. Also, my choice of clothes was extremely limited, as woollen sports clothes were about the only type of garment that looked at all suitable with high boots. Then, because I never looked really right, I wore inconspicuous, drab colours. A dark blue dress with a white collar was as dashing a garment as I ever put on. Now the revolution started. I wanted silk dresses, lots of silk dresses, plain silk and prints, and all must be colourful. This revolution was most expensive, and it went on for years.

There was one afternoon dress which I had at this time

that I particularly liked. I blush to say so, but it was practically orange in colour. I remember an extraordinarily nice colleague of mine saying, 'That's a nice bold colour, Lulie.' His use of the word 'bold' opened my eyes for a moment, and I thought, 'Maybe this colour is a little flamboyant, but I like it very much, and I enjoy wearing this dress.' So I went on wearing it.

After a while I tamed down on dresses a little, but for years my hats were unduly colourful. What I really liked was a bright blue hat with red and green feathers on it. I don't know what I looked like, but I enjoyed myself, and I thought, for the first time in years, that clothes were fun. About the middle of the second winter my right foot swelled up and was sore to walk on. I had to walk very slowly. I discussed with F. M. the possibility of consulting a doctor. He was not averse to it, and there were a good many doctors at hand who had had lessons themselves and who knew the work from the inside, and as a matter of direct experience. However, F. M. and I both felt that they would not have much to offer, as a process had been started and it would have to run its course. My foot stayed in this condition for about three weeks. Then the swelling and soreness left it and I walked much better and with more ease and comfort. I had not been at all disturbed by what had happened to my foot. In my first series of lessons when my back started aching I was frightened, but by this time I understood the work and had deep confidence in it, and it seemed quite reasonable that when a basic change came one would have to pay for it. This happens in other things, such as psychological changes, so I saw no reason why it shouldn't happen in this work.

Periodically, and for years, I would have manifestations of this sort. I have described the new HN & B pattern as a process—a righting process. When this pattern is operative, it appears to right the body in a steady, cumulative way, and at intervals this righting process mounts up, and then a basic change takes place. At such times I might have an uncomfortable manifestation as well as severe fatigue, but always after such a change I would be markedly improved in one form or another and have a considerable increase in strength and energy. This story of my own case is not representative of all pupils, as I was a badly handicapped person, and it is to the handicapped and those seriously out of kilter that such marked manifestations occur.

There were a number of other changes that took place as the course progressed. My right foot and leg were always much colder than my left foot and leg. This difference in temperature decreased to the point where it was barely discernible.

Also, my right foot used to blister continually. Now, although I was walking much more than I used to, it never blistered.

Prior to stormy weather my left foot and ankle, where tendons had been transplanted, would ache. Now it never ached at all, regardless of what weather came.

My condition was so improved that I was full of hope that my remaining difficulties would lessen too. This hope was accompanied by emotional impatience. I remember in particular that I was obsessively anxious for certain conditions in my shoulders to clear up, and I wanted them to clear up within a definite time limit, say March 13th, at three p.m. As long as I was in this state I could not work well, in fact, I could hardly work at all. My emotional desire for the end was always obtruding itself into my consciousness and making it difficult for me to focus on the various and separate steps (or means) necessary to achieve my end.

I went on butting my head against a stone wall this way for a long time. Finally, one day an inner change took place. I have always expressed it to myself by saying 'the old Adam died within me.' I looked at things with new eyes, and I worked in a different manner. Repeated failure had taught me that an active emotional interest in my objective or end would prevent me from ever reaching it. I had to 'give up'. No more thoughts about the final end, no more interest that way. If possible, be interested in the various steps comprising the method of attaining one's objective. If this is not possible, work on these steps with full consciousness as a matter of

Fig. 14. Lulie in 1952.

discipline. In this way detachment was born. In this way an ability to work independently and successfully came to me.

After this inner change in outlook my progress was much more rapid, and soon a second revolution was under way. I had a great desire to get into things, and to do things that I had never done before, or had done only in an inept and faltering way. World events were with me at this point. England had devalued the pound, and in consequence my finances were affected very favourably.

I decided to take riding lessons. I had always ridden on my grandfather's farm in North Carolina in an inept sort of way.

I had ridden a gentle horse and just walked and trotted. My balance in riding had been very poor. This made a strong grip doubly necessary, and I had had no grip at all. The right knee had always flapped away from the horse's side. Also, it had been extremely difficult to keep the right heel down (at that time my heel could not touch the floor when I stood). Because of my poor balance and grip I was apt to do that blasphemous thing called 'riding on the reins'. In England I now took ten riding lessons from an expert teacher. At the end of that time I was cantering and doing mild jumping. It sounds like a short time, and in an ordinary situation it would have been far too short a time, but my bodily conditions were so changed that my difficulties seemed to fall away from me with even a little help.

In the first place, I had a very good balance. The new HN & B pattern made all the difference there. Before, when my back was shortening and narrowing, my whole skeletal alignment was working against me, as this use of the back tended to throw my pelvis forward and my knees back. Now all was changed. My skeletal alignment was working for me. No unduly strong grip was needed, but I had a strong grip. The difference in the strength of a knee grip when a person is lengthening and widening the back, or shortening and narrowing the back (always in conjunction with the head, of course), is quite incredible. Also, my right heel would now stay down, and I no longer had the temptation to seek security by riding on the reins. Years later in the U.S. I acquired a pony that everyone in the neighbourhood considered would be too spirited for me. I was not at all sure myself that she wouldn't be, but due to the quality and lightness of my hands and a good balance I was able to ride her with control.

The next thing I went in for was dancing. I took some lessons in a funny little hall on the King's Road. A great many festivities were looming up that spring, the last spring of the course for me, and I wanted to participate fully in all of them. There was to be a wedding with a party afterwards. One of my colleagues was giving a dance, but most important of all, there was to be a Conference of the Associations of Commerce of the Empire. This Conference had a particular interest for me. A distant connection of mine by marriage, in fact, he was no connection at all except by close affection and adoption—I looked on him as a special uncle—was heading this Conference, and I had never seen him in public life. Then, a Canadian delegate to the Conference, whom I have always considered Canada's most attractive man, was taking me to all the parties.

I have to stop here and remember that the reader will want to know what success I had in dancing. In an odd way I had, to a great extent, lost interest in my 'improvements'. I had become interested in life—it was all opening up before me, and I simply wanted to enter more fully into living, so all I have to say about dancing is that at the first party, which was after the wedding, I had no difficulty at all. I went with a woman colleague of mine (who was excessively tall) and two men. At the end of the evening one of the men told me that he and his friend had been apprehensive as to how easy either of us would be to dance with, but to their surprise they had had no trouble whatsoever, and that it had been grand. He mentioned in particular the fact that we both followed so easily. This is a point always mentioned when the dancing of girls and women trained in the Alexander work is discussed.

Then came the festivities of the Conference. In preparation for the opening party of the Conference I went to Elizabeth Arden for the first time in my life. I remember distinctly seeing myself in a mirror after I had gone home and having a momentary sense of what was almost panic. I was looking at an unfamiliar personality. For a few moments I was bewildered and felt as if I had lost my moorings. Then I thought, 'Well, I like this new person that is me, and I am going to wear gold slippers and a flame-coloured chiffon dress bordered with a gold thread tonight. My uncle will have lots of ribbons and medals—big ones—on his shirt-front, and my escort will have some ribbons and medals too—little ones. The Duke of York will be there, and General Smuts, and maybe, just maybe, when my uncle proposes and drinks the health of the King, he will throw his champagne glass upon the floor. I do hope so.'

So ended my years of training in England.

Chapter 10

POSTSCRIPT TO THE TEACHER TRAINING COURSE

'What happened next,' the reader may ask, 'after the training course was over?' We all received certificates from F. M. qualifying us to teach. About half of the original group of students remained at Ashley Place for a few years and worked for F. M. The rest went out and taught independently. Four members of my own group and one member of the other group are the only ones from the first training course who have continued working as teachers; the rest have turned to other occupations.

I returned to the United States at the end of the course, teaching there independently in the winters and returning to London in summers to work with my colleagues. I did this every summer until the war broke out, with the exception of two summers when colleagues visited me.

We worked on our own teaching problems, building in our skill, and we also worked with the new students in the training course.

I thus had first-hand experience with all teacher training courses from February 1931 to September 1938. These new students worked under highly favourable conditions. In addition to two hours of work with F. M. in the morning, they had the skilled help of graduate teachers in the afternoons. Many competent teachers were turned out in these days, but alas! these favourable conditions did not last. As time went on more and more graduate teachers left Ashley Place, so there was less help for the students. Also F. M. gave them less time. I remember going over one summer shortly after Aldous Huxley had had lessons. Huxley had given F. M. some very good publicity and as a result pupils were storming the doors of 16 Ashley Place. F. M. was taking his students for one hour a day, and the hour was not scheduled in advance. The students would come to Ashley Place in the morning and hang around until the secretary could tell them when F. M. would hold their class.

But even under these conditions some of the group learned to be teachers. A self-resourceful student with a detached and realistic outlook on F. M. and help from a competent graduate teacher could always learn.

From 1939 on I had no direct connection with the training courses in London.

What of F. M. during this period?

Friends have asked me, 'Wasn't he interested in what you were doing in the United States?' No, he did not like to hear what I or anyone else was doing as a teacher. (The situation may have changed in his last years—I can speak only of my own experience in the years when I had close contact with him.) But once you accepted this, he was very nice indeed. You had the run of the place—you felt that you were welcome there.

It was the personal rather than the professional aspect that F. M. emphasized in his relationship to his teachers. He was fond of us and glad to have us around, provided we understood the rules of the game. The rules seemed to be these: we must present no problems, ask no help, and we must not disagree with him. We must also manage not to stand out too clearly in his consciousness as teachers of his work.

As long as such a régime was followed we were all very happy together. In these early days of teaching such a programme could be more or less adhered to, but as time went on troubles arose between F. M. and some of his teachers. There was always a small group, however, who were his Greek chorus, his undiscriminating worshippers, who took him as their hero symbol throughout his life.

I know of only two instances in which Alexander explicitly discredited his teachers, but in an indirect way he did cast doubt on the professional ability of a number of them. 'X', he would say, 'taught all right while he was here; I don't know what he is doing now.' It was his tone rather than his words that gave the implication, and in the instances that I knew of personally it was on the competent teachers that he cast such doubts.

I fared better than the others (there was an ocean between us), though F. M. never recommended any American pupils to me. When American enquirers wrote and asked for the names of Alexander teachers in the U.S., the reply from Ashley Place after A. R. Alexander's death was that there were no teachers in this country. I have three such letters in my files brought to me by puzzled Americans. F. M. had always possessed a certain ostrich-like quality but never more so than in this instance, when on the one hand his letters denied my professional existence, and on the other hand in his introduction to *The Universal Constant in Living* he mentions my name and thanks me for my professional work in New York and in the South.

What of his other human contacts at this time? His relationship with Peggy, his adopted daughter, who was now a young girl, was not so close as it used to be when she was a child. They no longer went on holidays together. It may have been simply because she wanted to do different things at that age, or it may have been that while F. M. could have a most happy companionship with a child, difficulties would creep in as the child grew up and the requirements of the relationship changed. F. M. went alone on his holidays for a few years. Later on there was a little boy he took with him; again it was a child he wanted. In an adult relationship there might come the need to give and take that would be difficult for him.

There were two women F. M. was close to in these days. Unlike his wife, both of these women looked on his work with the deepest admiration. The first woman, who unfortunately died, had a motherly, feminine quality about her, yet she was at the same time practical, executive, and capable. She got along easily and comfortably with other people.

The second woman struck one as looking on F. M.'s work as if it were as important as life itself. She had much to offer him in the way of appreciation and understanding, and seemingly she too found human relationships a challenge.

During the years of the Second World War F. M. made

another visit to the United States. Here the usual cycle started. He acquired some new pupils and, as always, he impressed them very much with what he could do for them. And as usual a few of these new pupils hopefully struggled to further his work and secure contacts with influential people for him. But the old supporters, including John Dewey who still took lessons himself, no longer tried to do this. Experience seemed to have taught them it was like butting one's head against a stone wall to work for any project that would make Alexander's work become better known and more authoritatively accepted. A great many of his old pupils, however, who had ardently supported him on his previous visits to the United States did not return to him for lessons this time. I talked to many of these people as I was interested to know why they had not come back. A number of them said that it boiled down to going to him for very expensive lessons and then there was nothing they could do about it themselves; if they attempted to work by themselves, they lost the benefits of his work more rapidly than if they did nothing. It was the old story of his verbal inadequacy in communication.

A number of others had discovered that Alexander had feet of clay, and they were unable to consider the man and his work as separate things. Because they mistrusted certain things about the man, they became uncertain about his work.

He returned to England a few years before the war ended, and I never saw him again.

Important happenings in the work, however, were reported to me by colleagues. One of these was the Alexander Libel Action in South Africa.*

In 1944 Dr E. Jokl, the physical education officer of the South African Government, published a strong attack on Alexander's method of re-education. Alexander asked for the withdrawal of the article, and when this was refused, he sued for defamation. The case came up for trial in Johannesburg before Mr Justice Clayden in 1948. Judgment was given for

---

* These facts are taken from an article by Dr Wilfred Barlow called 'The Alexander Libel Action', printed in *The Lancet*, July 1, 1960.

Postscript to the Teacher Training Course

Alexander, and this was confirmed in 1949 at the Supreme Court of Appeal. The Appeal Judges of the Supreme Court said there was malevolence in the article and that it was not 'a dispassionate scientific analysis of the theories and claims in Alexander's books'.

It was also during this period that the War Office approached F. M. to see if his technique could not be used in the training of the Army. This was one opportunity that I knew of that really could not be followed up. Obviously there were not teachers enough to train an army. The offer, however, indicates how highly his work was regarded.

Colleagues also told me of Sir Stafford Cripps's attempts to form an Alexander Society. Sir Stafford and Lady Cripps had become ardent pupils of Alexander's work and Sir Stafford was unflagging in his efforts to further the work and safeguard its future. He was particularly anxious that an Alexander Society be formed that would promote and safeguard professional standards among the teachers. It would also be a central organization to whom the public could turn for information concerning teachers. This very worthwhile project failed. F. M.'s remark (which I have already quoted) when Sir Stafford read his plan of organization was: 'Why, under this scheme I could be outvoted!' A colleague who was present told me that Sir Stafford replied: 'After all, F. M., we do live in a democratic country.'

With no qualifications for prospective teachers and no control organization safeguarding standards among graduate teachers, a chaotic situation inevitably arose. A group of teachers came into being that might well be called the 'splinter' group inasmuch as they are as so many individual splinters breaking off from the main tree. To the best of my knowledge there has been no statement from any individual of this group as to how he differs from Alexander or what he believes his individual contribution to be. I asked one of them to discuss this with me once, but he demurred. While they are not communicative as to definite specific differences, the majority of them hold that they have a certain unprecedented mastery of words that enables them to teach this most difficult 'skill' to people in a very short time. One woman reported that a London group a few summers ago taught her—as a pupil—'everything there was to know' in two weeks. A young woman in New York City claims to train teachers in about one-tenth of the time that such work actually requires. Generally the theme is 'you can do it chiefly through words and we for the first time have found the words.'

A few 'splinter' teachers go down bizarre pathways; they use electric vibrators on the head, tennis balls on the arms (to produce relaxation, they say), and a colleague reported to me that one has attempted to teach through correspondence. In my experience with the few 'splinter' teachers who have put their hands on me, I have found that they were not manually able to get the new HN & B pattern working; they had indeed small conception of what it involved. In their teaching they had left out Alexander's great discovery and were pawning off on the public comparatively trivial inventions of their own. When this kind of thing happens, the reputation of the technique inevitably suffers. Even in his lifetime Alexander was not able to prevent this desiccation and distortion of his work.

Since Alexander's death in 1955, however, some constructive counter forces have come to life calculated to protect both the technique and the public. There are more teachers being trained in a competent and responsible manner than ever before. There has also been formed a Society of Alexander Teachers, one of the main functions of which is to promote and ensure standards of professional competency among teachers.

We have all of us heard the saying that a new truth will manage to survive despite all difficulties, and certainly the strange story of Alexander's work bears this out. It is even hard to enumerate, because of their great number, the well-nigh insuperable obstacles that had to be met to ensure the work's survival. Yet they were met, and now, nine years after Alexander's death, one can say truthfully that his work has never been in so favourable a position and so strongly entrenched.

Chapter 11

MY TEACHING EXPERIENCE IN NEW YORK CITY

My four years of training with all their gaiety and happiness, their doubt and anxiety, their discipline and final achievement, were over. I began to teach. Although in my first few years I made teaching visits to various places (New Orleans, Louisiana; Highlands, North Carolina; Richmond, Virginia; Mansfield, Ohio; and Montreal, Canada), the main story of my teaching experience takes place in New York City. I started teaching there in 1937. I have often been asked how on earth I got started in New York. Happily, my first two pupils came to me; I did not have to seek them out. One of them was an Englishman who knew of me through an English colleague; the other one had heard of me through Mrs Brown. It was fortunate that my first two pupils came this way, as salesmanship had been left out of my make-up. Once I had my start, salesmanship was not so necessary, as the work, if given a chance, will sell itself. Other contacts came to me through my first pupils. Soon the young man brought a young woman. She had come because of tension. After holding her stomach in conscientiously for a long time, the front of her pelvis was sticking out so prominently that holes were worn on the linings of her coats where the pelvis rubbed against them. This young woman caused me one of my most embarrassing professional moments. She asked me respectfully if I could fit her in. I thought of my clean blank appointment book and had a strong desire to laugh. But I controlled myself, and with a serious face gave her some appointments, and so we started.

As I look back on those first years, my efforts seem focused on becoming more proficient as a teacher rather than on obtaining pupils. A. R. Alexander had come to the United States to teach one year before I graduated. He lived in Boston but came to New York every weekend to teach. To my surprise and disappointment he proceeded to discredit me as a teacher as soon as I arrived in New York. Knowing A. R. as well as I did, I cannot see now why I was surprised. He had F. M.'s weaknesses, and he was far more insecure. I remember a rather poignant illustration of this: in the early days when I once went out to dinner with him he said with some pride that every waiter in that restaurant respected him now, as he always gave them large bills to change! So, despite his great manual skill, experience, and backing from F. M., he must have regarded me as a potential threat rather than as a supporting ally.

I was greatly distressed by A. R.'s behaviour, as I had looked forward to his professional companionship. Especially I had hoped that the mistakes made in England would not be repeated here, that A. R. would not rouse the distrust and antagonism of old and staunch supporters of the work, and that all Alexander's teachers could work co-operatively together and present a united front to the outside world. However, this was not to be.

The small group of American pupils whom already knew were outraged by A. R.'s behaviour and went out of their way to give me support, coming to me themselves and recommending me to their friends. A very large family from the Midwest asked me to come out to them for a month every spring and fall and said they would get me all the pupils I could teach, as indeed they did. This gave me a financial backlog in those early years so that I could be perfectly carefree.

My pupils were my own and had not been baffled by the initial instructions of either Alexander. Because of my difficulties as a student in not understanding what F. M. wanted me to do, I was extremely desirous to make the initial instructions as to procedure clear to my pupils. This does not mean that I minimized the use of hands in any way. I was simply trying to handle the verbal side of the work more adequately. My efforts were well rewarded, and while a few pupils managed to tie themselves up in verbal difficulties and intellectualizations and more than a few persistently continued to 'feel' things out, a large number fulfilled my hopes. They were increasingly able to carry out instructions and to gain understanding.

However, difficulties of an unexpected nature arose in teaching. One of my greatest problems was the opposition between the pupil's intellectual beliefs and his actual beliefs. The actions of the pupil give me the clue to his real beliefs. He does not believe that the HN & B pattern can be made operative by a sequence of thoughts. Instead of thinking, he tries by adroit shoves, squirms, and movements to make the pattern work, and far from looking upon feeling as an unreliable guide, it is the only thing to which he gives validity. If he works sixty seconds and doesn't get the kind of feeling he thinks he should have, he says that nothing is happening, and often his very notion of the work is to conjure up certain feelings.

When a person has held beliefs for a number of years, they have become habits of thought. They cannot be changed by talk, argument, or even by several demonstrations. Repeated demonstrations are needed. A real change comes when experience builds up and builds up so that the pupil finally *knows* the HN & B pattern. As Archibald MacLeish says in his book *Poetry and Experience*,* man can 'know' the world, not by exegesis or demonstration or proofs but directly, as a man knows 'apple in his mouth'. In short, it is the union between the knowledge of the fact and the experience of the fact. Only then is the old outlook obliterated.

Another very serious difficulty for the teacher is a semantic one. New wine is put in old bottles. Familiar words are used to express unfamiliar experiences. The words *neck free, head up* (leaving out forward), *back lengthening* (generally leaving out the widening) are used in certain fields of medicine, in osteopathy, and a number of other systems that handle the body. When pupils first hear these words from an Alexander teacher, they often say, 'Oh, yes, what you teach is like osteopathy, or exercises, or traction, etc.' They cannot realize that familiar words stand for experiences very different from the ones they have always associated with these words. To

---
* Houghton Mifflin Co.

take one example, consider the word 'up'. When there is a locking of the head on the neck, and the head is taken up by thought, by pulling, by shoving, by any method whatsoever, the word 'up' stands for an experience completely different from that meant by the same word when the head has been unlocked from the neck as it is in Alexander's work. In the new HN & B pattern, the step 'head forward in relation to the neck' unlocks the head on the neck, and the 'up' that follows brings to the pupil a new experience, an unfamiliar bodily condition. The teacher finds, however, that the pupil is continually reverting to his original notion of 'up'. Soon in teaching one finds oneself really up against the 'battle of the mind', and one needs as much intelligence and patience as one can muster to help the pupil to a new outlook.

It is what actually happens in a lesson, however, that gives the meat of one's teaching experience, and it is in lessons that one gets constantly repeated corroboration of F. M.'s principles and techniques. I give here an account of two lessons which illustrate the characteristic of the HN & B pattern: that of righting the other parts of the body. These lessons show how the operation of the HN & B pattern visibly straightened a twisted ankle and caused a heel unable to touch the floor to drop.

Account of Two Lessons with Susan

Susan is a young girl of about 14 who had been badly affected by polio.

October 6th
   Susan is lying on the table. I am taking her head forward and up. Her knees are propped up on pillows.
   Susan: My ankle is nearly killing me. (Her right ankle.)
   L.W.: What do you mean?
   Susan: It is trying to pull itself straight. (Her ankle was badly twisted.)
   I went down and put my hand on it. I could feel it trying to right itself. I could also see a faint cumulative straightening

process going on. However, when Susan stopped giving the thoughts to the HN & B pattern, the impulses in the ankle stopped abruptly.

October 8th

Susan is sitting in a chair in front of a mirror, her feet on a box. As always, her right heel was up about two inches from the box, and her right ankle was twisted, although slightly less twisted than it had been at the beginning of the last lesson. I put my hands on her head, taking it forward and up a number of times. Then I put my hands on her back and lengthened and widened it a number of times.

'Now, Susan,' I said, 'I am going to move you backward and forward on the hips. Right now I am going to take you forward. Your job is to inhibit* going forward. That is, you must have a continually renewed decision to do nothing about going forward, and you must also, after each decision, give the thoughts to the HN & B pattern. In this way your body will be on an entirely new pattern while you are moving.'

Susan, who was a very good worker, inhibited and gave the thoughts to the HN & B pattern. We kept up this procedure as I moved her forward and backward on the hip—tiny movements, about half an inch forward and then backward.

Suddenly Susan said, 'Look at my foot in the mirror!'

I looked. We both saw the slow, steady movement in the foot, the heel dropping and the ankle straightening.

'That's objective evidence for you,' said Susan. 'I wish Dr X had seen that last year.' We continued to work. She lay on the table for a bit, and we worked there, strengthening the HN & B pattern, and then returned to the chair. We looked in the mirror and saw that her heel was considerably closer to touching the base of the box and that her ankle was straighter than before we had worked on the table.

The operation of the HN & B pattern, in these two lessons, *visibly* righted the specific parts, the connection between cause and effect being *observable*.

---

* See Chapter 15 on inhibition, p. 152.

The following is an account of how an eleven-year-old girl and myself worked out some of her writing difficulties together. In order to understand these lessons the reader must have read the chapter on inhibition, page 152.

ACCOUNT OF TEACHING NORA

Nora was having a hard time with her school work on account of her writing. Her letters were so tiny as to be almost infinitesimal, and they were likewise very laboured and strained. She had had Alexander lessons with me twice a week for about three months. She was a good thinker and had reached the stage where she could get the new head, neck and back pattern going by herself.

One morning when she arrived I noticed that the alignment of her arms had decidedly improved, and I decided that it was now time to start applying what she had learned in her lessons to writing.

We began by having her sit down in front of a table with a pad on it and take up a pencil. She gripped the pencil so violently that one wondered how she could move her fingers at all. The tininess of her writing was explained at once: only very restricted movement was possible with such a grip. As she moved her torso towards the table, she twisted her back markedly.

'Nora,' I said, 'let's try that again. You see, we want this head, neck and back pattern to go on while you are writing. I'll take your head and give you a little help, but you must continue to think the thoughts to the head, neck and back while I move you forward to the table.'

We did this successfully. As she came forward to the table she was lengthening and widening her back, and she was not twisting it.

We repeated this same procedure when she picked up the pencil. She held the pencil somewhat insecurely but with a gentle rather than a violent grip. She was not asked to hold it gently. She had been told to hold it any way she could, provided the new head, neck and back pattern was working.

'Now, Nora, write your name,' I said.

With this she got into trouble at once and reverted to the old pattern. We repeated the procedure several times, but the results were no better.

'Nora,' I said, 'in spite of all our preparation, the minute you attempt to write you fail. Now that is exactly what Alexander was up against when he tried to speak. He found that if he so much as thought about speaking, it was impossible for him to speak in a new or different way. And if you think about writing you will not be able to use your new muscular pattern when you write. So we are not going to think about writing just now. We are not going to write; we are going to draw shapes instead.'

She got the point, and before each lesson, for a while, she would draw two or three simple shapes—a circle, a square, a triangle, or something such as that. It is sometimes better to let a pupil—adult or child—try to keep the head, neck and back pattern going and write well and see for themselves it can't be done, rather than to tell him there is an inseparable fusion between the idea of writing and the old muscular pattern of writing and that to get rid of the old pattern they will have to get rid of the idea. The pupil simply will not believe you and can only be convinced by going through the experience of trying to write well with the head, neck and back pattern going and finding it impossible.

While Nora drew shapes, I had my hands on her head, checking up on whether she was keeping the HN & B pattern going or not, and telling her that I didn't care what she did in the way of making nice circles, etc., that simply she was to use her hands in any way she could, provided she kept the new pattern going.

We never worked at this long. We did a short bit—a very short bit—of disciplined work before each lesson. The way was somewhat tortuous at first. Nora's shapes were so lightly drawn as to be barely visible, and they also tended to be very tiny. I got a lined pad and told her to make them at least two lines high. She did this rather successfully, although after she had been at it for a minute or two the shapes would have a way of relapsing into tininess. Gradually, however, they did so less and less. And gradually the shapes began to be normally visible. She had begun to be less uncertain in her new control.

Then she drew a simple cat on a fence, like this. Actually, to draw the cat, she had to make the letter V upside down (the cat's ears), the letter O (the cat's body and head), and the letter S (the cat's tail). However, in her mind she was drawing, not writing, and so as the old idea was not there she was not dragged back into her old habits as she made the letters.

She seemed, by now, as she used her hands and arms, to have started a new neuromuscular pattern, and

Fig. 15. Nora's cat drawing.

I thought it was time to risk being bold. I asked her to make letters, definite letters, O, R, V, and so forth. The only conditions were that she was to use her hand and arm as a subordinate part of her new head, neck and back pattern, and the letters must be at least two lines high. If she relapsed into her old writing habits, we could give up letters and go back to shapes. However, she did not relapse. She made three large, well-shaped, flowing letters.

The fight is not over yet. Nora says that at school her writing relapses: that the idea of writing is in her mind and brings back her old habits. A child can seldom be taught under ideal conditions, and at the moment she is making headway in achieving a new control during her Alexander lessons.

I would like to give one other example of the prime importance of getting rid of the 'idea' of an activity for one to be able to get rid of the wrong pattern of that activity. It occurred to me in my own student days that it would be much easier to get rid of the idea of walking if one walked backwards. I tried this out and was greatly encouraged by the results. The great advantage of walking backwards was that it made the inhibition so much easier. Taking a step backwards was different from taking a step forward both in concept and feeling. It was not one's idea of walking, and it did not feel like walking. The battle was half over even before one started. Later, as a teacher, when I was taking pupils who had had infantile paralysis, I would have those who had reached the stage when they could apply the work to walking back in this way. Sometimes a pupil with polio could take a step backwards without the vestige of a limp while the same pupil taking a step forward would retain a limp. The limp was no longer necessitated by the pupil's physiological condition but occurred because the inhibition had broken down, so that the idea of walking was there, and the old habit of walking was again operative.

In my pupils I noticed the same associated changes that I had seen take place in my fellow students in the training course. And I observed some additional associated changes, probably because I scrutinized my own pupils more intently and also because I was now better qualified to observe.

In the majority of cases the *skin* is much improved. It becomes clearer and is a better colour.

The *eyes* become more alive and more alert. Dull, dead looking eyes disappear, and as a consequence a number of pupils are better-looking and more arresting in appearance.

Improvement in *eyesight* sometimes occurs. A short time ago I was teaching a young girl. She was sitting in a chair in front of a mirror. I was taking her head forward and up. She said, 'When I first came into this room and sat down, I could not see my eyes in the mirror—they were only sockets. Now I can see the eyes—they are blue, and with pupils!'

This same young girl after lessons two or three times a week for nearly a year (with another teacher) had an improvement in eye correction of one-third per cent. The oculist did not know how to account for it.

Another pupil who came to me because of eyestrain said:

> When I first looked into the mirror there was a grey cloud in the centre part of vision of my left eye. In the last four

days since my lessons there has been a steady improvement. The fog has almost cleared. I don't see a cloud any more, just an ordinary eye with the pupil.

E.B.

More saliva is secreted. When the HN & B pattern has become strongly established in a lesson, one of the first things the teacher is apt to notice is that the pupil swallows more— he is swallowing excess saliva. The pupil is not generally conscious of this phenomenon, and the swallowing only goes on for a moment or so. It is interesting to note that the new HN & B pattern thus affects the functioning of the salivary gland.

Another very interesting happening took place in the case of a pupil who had suffered from angina pectoris. He writes:

> I had not had an attack for some time when I commenced treatment, but I had consistently felt the slight teasing pain in the palm of my left hand which is a typical symptom of angina. This disappeared completely after the first treatment and has not reappeared [years later].

S.B.

Quite often in my observations of pupils the releasing of muscle tensions seem to have a favourable effect upon peripheral circulation.

A child of nine, badly affected by polio, came to me for lessons. She was in such bad shape that nothing seemed to happen in her lessons for quite a long time, but we had some assurance, almost at once, that an important thing was happening to her circulation. Her lesson was in the morning, and in the early evening every day she would have a sudden warming rush of blood to her right leg and foot (these had always been cold and clammy).

There was a young woman with polio who came for lessons and who had considerable discomfort and pain in the lower back. During lessons, after the HN & B pattern had been strongly built up, she would have a rush of blood to the lower back.

I had a pupil who was having considerable trouble with his right foot. It was cold in temperature, normal functioning was becoming more and more difficult, and he was having increasing pain. I quote from his remarks:

> For many years I had been suffering from pain and discomfort in my right foot. Different supports in the shoe only temporarily afforded relief. At night considerable massaging was necessary to bring circulation into the foot. Heat therapy had afforded no remedy. . . I began to take lessons. . . . As time went on the condition in my foot changed. I now have no pain in walking and I do not use any special support in the right shoe. Circulation has come into my foot and massaging it is no longer necessary.
>
> L.C.

I have another man pupil now, who, in the first minute or so of his lessons, when he is sitting on a chair giving the thoughts to the head, neck and back, and I am, with my hands, aiding the head going forward and up, says: 'Now the blood has rushed to my right foot and it's hot'; and then shortly, 'Now my left foot is hot.' (G.D.)

Another effect of lessening tensions is the *disappearance of sore spots* in the back. Many pupils have these spots. I asked a doctor what process actually took place when these spots disappeared. He said involuntary muscles under continuous tension (spasm) usually will be sore, and the disappearance of soreness is evidence of the release of tension or spasm.

There are a number of systems that bring relief from tension. Pupils who have used the systems and found them helpful agree, however, that the degree and quality of the relief they find in Alexander's work is different from anything they have hitherto experienced. The Alexander work changes the basic body pattern, and this brings about a more complete freedom from tensions than systems which aim at producing relaxation in specific parts.

Very tense pupils sometimes find the relief brought about by Alexander's work so great that they find it difficult to stay awake during a lesson. If they do manage to stay awake, they will often fall into a deep sleep after a lesson. Their behaviour frequently changes as tension lessens. Adults who have a somewhat obsessive need to talk become quiet. Children who are intractable become co-operative. Linked up with the decrease of tension is the *increase of tranquillity*. Most pupils become much more tranquil.

Now as to *structural changes*: The HN & B pattern tends to right skeletal alignment and structural defects. There are, however, conditions under which it does not do so. I refer to such conditions as actual muscle impairment, surgical fixation, and such pronounced muscular imbalance as results in rotated vertebrae.

In my own case many structural defects have been righted but others still remain.

One is always hearing remarks such as this from pupils: 'Look at my legs—they are almost entirely straight. I used to be so knock-kneed.'

The power of the HN & B pattern to remove structural defects is conditioned by the nature and causes of these defects.

I have often been asked to what extent the work affects nervous and emotional difficulties. Here too one cannot make a generalization. I have seen a great many personality changes; in these instances the psychic difficulties are not entrenched enough to be able to withstand the progressive changes in the organism caused by the operation of the HN & B pattern. But this is not always the case. Sometimes the psychic difficulties are so entrenched that they make it well nigh impossible for a pupil to learn the technique.

There are some excellent photographic records, as well as accounts, of structural and other changes resulting from Alexander's work in the pamphlets of Dr Wilfred Barlow.* I have often been asked what kinds of difficulties led my pupils to try Alexander's work. I can answer at once: a very wide range of difficulties—such things as flat feet, sciatica, back

---

* 'Anxiety and Muscle Tension', reprinted from *Modern Trends in Psychosomatic Medicine*, published by Butterworth & Co., London. 'Psychosomatic Problems in Postural Education,' *The Lancet*, September 24, 1955. 'Anxiety and Muscle-Tension Pain,' *British Journal of Clinical Practice*, May, 1959.

troubles of various sorts. An insurance salesman came so that he might have more strength to tramp the streets and sell; a businessman came to get relief from tension. Pregnant women came so that they might have an easier labour, and also to enable them to carry their children more easily before labour. Piano students and voice students came so as to meet more proficiently some of the technical problems of their profession, such things as tone, power, range of notes, etc.

As a part of my teaching experience I am including a few letters and remarks from pupils describing what the work has meant to them as a human experience and how it has met certain needs in their lives. A pupil who is an artist tells of a change produced by the work which is seldom mentioned, although it always takes place: an aesthetic change. If anyone had asked me what was the matter with this pupil, I would have been hard put to it for an answer. From the ordinary person's point of view there was nothing the matter with her, because no one symptom stood out and called for a remedy. From our point of view there was well nigh everything the matter with her. Her head was retracted back from her neck so violently that it was not possible to get the new HN & B pattern fully and powerfully operative for some time. Mainly she suffered from an ever-mounting exhaustion. She herself says that it was becoming increasingly difficult for her to think with any clarity. Here is her letter:

> There is a full-length mirror in my room and often just before I go to bed at night I look at myself. I see the same harmony and balance and strength that is shown in the compositional balance of a great drawing.
>
> I see an aesthetic thing operating here, there is a basic correctness of line. The line of the leg is different, the foot, the neck, the wrists, the arms.
>
> It gives me a deep sense of confidence that these changes have been effected at such an age—fifty years. It doesn't bother me to think of being sixty because I look and feel younger now than I did at forty. I have a renewed interest in using my body. I can walk further, swim further than I could a few years ago. I can climb my stairs (three flights) without

feeling them any more; a few years ago I had to gird my loins to do it. Recently I was in Montreal at a business party. "I could have danced all night" but my contemporaries were pegged out. . . . I have a renewed interest in wanting to use my body—to dance, to swim, to walk, to simply move. Even such household chores as washing my clothes, which I used to find exhausting, I do not mind any more.

In letters or conversation she frequently mentioned increased ability to think clearly. I quote one letter:

> You did me so much good last time—I can't tell you—my brain seems to get clearer and clearer. Clarification comes without any effort—it goes on, as it were, spontaneously.
>
> *D. M.*

The following is a letter from a pupil—a young girl in her twenties—who had had a serious riding accident. She had fallen during a jump, and the horse had rolled on her neck. It was a number of years after the accident before her mother heard of me and brought her to me for lessons. She had tried various therapies but with small success. She had literally no energy and a constantly mounting fatigue. Walking and standing were particularly exhausting for her. She was also nervously irritable to a marked degree and easily discouraged. I quote her letter:

> It gives me so darn much pleasure to think about you and the work—and especially to hear that you are going to write a book—somebody's got to!
>
> As for the work itself—goodness, I remember as though it was yesterday being brought in to see you—sulky and furious—and I am sure all you took in about me was my frightful posture and the dragging tensions. You looked at me exactly as though I were an ailing horse, stood me up, tried to jog loose my knees*—which were locked—you shook your head and I guess almost decided not to attempt the case. Don't know what decided you to go ahead, but you did. That first week was practically a battle of wills. I didn't see how anything could change my posture, after all those

---

* The locking of the knees indicates a certain condition of the back.

years of being told to hold up my shoulders, I didn't understand what you were trying to do to me—putting me on my back on the floor with my head on a couple of books. And I didn't even start trying to quit being obstinate until I discovered there were things I simply couldn't do—like balance my knees where you had put them. That challenged me, and when I really began to listen to what you were saying, and got an inkling of how hard it would be to follow your instructions, I entered a new world of self-discipline—one in which the familiar feelings were invariably wrong, the neutral ground of no pushing was almost unattainable, and only the faintest glimmer of the possible new felicity of physical being was visible. Again and again—and again—just to get back to that plateau of letting things happen—I discovered how hard it is to quit forcing. You would say 'neck free, head forward and up' and in an effort to make my neck be free and my head *go* forward and up, I would send—not nerve impulses—but muscular impulses—and once more we would have to let it all drop before you began your interminable coaxing.*

That coaxing. [I should say manual coaxing.] It was one of the marvels of my life. It was as though with your hands you were appealing to some force within me which would understand your message much better than my mere mind could, and—if I would just keep clear of it and not mess it up—would obey you in spite of me. And finally I did learn at least to keep clear. After that, things began to happen—in the most astonishing ways. I fell apart. Literally—quite as though I had been held up by a superstructure of tension and muscle and energy (and, of course, I had—which made it tiresome—just to remain standing up) and when we hit the level of not forcing, all that supporting business fell away and there was nothing to hold me up. Like a person who has sustained nerve damage, I found all the familiar motion patterns strange, and felt I could barely walk.

Gradually the new, and correct, nerve impulses began to follow the paths suggested by the coaxing hands, and other queer manifestations came about. For several days I had a severe crick in the neck and found it difficult to hold my head up. Then all at once, as I walked down the street, I got

---

* She was 'doing' rather than 'thinking'.

the total impact of your long, patient re-education—it was an explosion, a high fierce peak of marvellous being—I was not walking, not touching the ground, I was floating, and no effort was needed to move me forward. I have never known anything like it, and in a state of exhilaration I just kept walking—for the sheer joy of it. The battle isn't over, and never will be. The orders are firmly enough established to keep me functioning reasonably well, but I don't work at them faithfully enough to float all the time.

B.J.

This letter tells in her own words the long slow struggle that was necessary to get the new HN & B pattern strongly established; it also illustrates the marked and occasionally dramatic manifestations that sometimes accompany the progress of a person seriously out of kilter. A particularly important emphasis in this letter is that on discipline. She says, 'I entered a new world of self-discipline' and 'I don't work at them faithfully enough to keep floating all the time.' It is well for the reader to know that even when a dramatic change has occurred it takes disciplined work to establish and increase this change. I think, though, that this pupil is a little hard on herself. She carries on the work well, and she is meeting a life involving hard physical labour most ably.

This letter brings out many new aspects of what Alexander work does for people:

November 16, 1958
It is hard to keep from sounding like a 'before and after' testimonial about the Alexander Technique.

Before I came to you for lessons I was in pain most of the time, taking many aspirins for backaches and headaches. Whenever I bent my back, even getting out of bed each morning, when making beds, picking up things from the floor, bending over work tables or sink, I almost always had to straighten up my back with help. I would push or pull myself back to normal against the nearest firm piece of furniture. (I had known from the time I was nineteen years old that I had a faulty joint in my left hip—diagnosed as a prenatal abnormality—causing one leg to be about two inches shorter than the other and creating a curvature in my spine.)

I had been told by an orthopaedic specialist to have my left shoes built up to take care of this discrepancy. This I had done continuously for nearly twenty years, but this had by no means solved my problem or done away with my difficulties.

That first month of daily half-hour lessons will always mark a personal revolution for me. I soon began to feel small differences. Almost at once I felt aches in newly awakened muscles. I slept more and with diminishing pain during the night. Soon I could sleep comfortably on my back which I had not been able to do for years.

Since I walked a mile and a half to my lessons and home afterwards, I made immediate use of what you were teaching me, in walking. My walk changed from one with a bounce to a smooth, comfortable, effortless walk which I enjoyed.

The small amount of theory you gave me at first was not as unfamiliar as I had expected it to be. I recognized certain similarities to the principles of art which I was studying at that time. The most outstanding of these stressed the need for integration; for the avoidance of domination by one part over another. I sensed a similarity to Alexander's principles from the beginning. My art teacher gave me rules of order in art; Alexander offered me rules of order for the body.

Unexpected improvements continued as my lessons went on, such as the ability to stand for hours at some job, without tiring, and to play the piano with much greater technical ease than I had been able to previously. And now, with no resulting aches.

I now began deliberately to apply the Alexander Technique to playing the piano. I did this every day for at least half an hour. In a few weeks a marked difference took place in my playing, but far more important than that was the improvement I noticed in everything I did because of the regular daily reinforcement of the new pattern I was learning. It was delightful that this could happen through my favourite pastime.

Friends continually asked 'What are those exercises you do that keep you so full of energy?' Though I denied any exercises I began to know that all my household chores, the walking and standing I do on my job, the different way of breathing had actually become the natural exercise my body needed. Now the bending, stretching, pulling and pushing, reaching high and reaching low were doing my muscles good. I felt best on the day I did the thorough housecleaning.

I can no longer sit, stand, lie, walk or work in the wrong way without becoming conscious almost at once of the faulty use of my body. It becomes necessary for me to change my position.

If I had had no specific handicap I would never have found my way to you at all and would not have fulfilled as fully as I now have some of my potentialities as a person.

What I'm really saying is that though most people find the Alexander Technique because of a specific disorder, people with no disorders could increase their potential for giving to life and partaking of life by knowing how to use their bodies.

With deepest respect and admiration,

Sincerely,
M.F.

The application of Alexander's work to sports and the victory over old habits, as mentioned in this letter, is particularly interesting.

My husband and I have worked together, in classes with you, then using what we have learned we have worked on by ourselves between our six-monthly visits. This has proved a great advantage as we have been able to share our understanding of the physical and mental changes which the work has brought about in each of us.

One of the techniques I have tried to learn is to 'meet the unexpected without tension'; by maintaining an easy balance in whatever position in space the body may happen to be. Applying this idea to sports, in my case badminton, or in any game where co-ordinations of eye and body are essential, is a fascinating exercise.

To play well you must never force or allow the speed or unexpectedness of any shot to throw you off balance, but maintain a smooth easiness of body and mind, however fast the game becomes. When one's back is lengthening and widening this is much easier to do as there is just one's normal weight to cope with and not weight plus pressure. The knees and legs are therefore able to move more freely and quickly in any direction. The calm awareness which is produced by the use of this technique makes for a greater control which you can depend on and re-establish during play, by running lightly through the orders.

Applying these techniques will not make you a champion if you are not equipped to be one, but it makes for an awareness of the co-ordinated one-ness of your body which you can use in every activity.

But the greatest change of all which an understanding and application of your work has given me is the knowledge, both theoretical and practical, that my long-standing habits of body and mind can be changed even in middle life. That the enormous tyranny of habit can, with steady application, be understood and changed.

B. D.

This letter covers ably and comprehensively the many different kinds of help that this work gives.

The work of F. M. Alexander first came to my notice in 1938 when I read Aldous Huxley's *Ends and Means*, in which there are two provocative references to it. The first of these speaks of it as giving 'relief from strain due to mal-adjustment, and consequent improvement in physical and mental health; increased consciousness of the physical means employed to gain the ends proposed by the will and, along with this, a general heightening of consciousness in all levels; a technique of inhibition, working on the physical level to prevent the body from slipping back, under the influence of greedy "end-gaining", into its old habits of mal-co-ordination, and working (by a kind of organic analogy) to inhibit undesirable impulses and irrelevance on the emotional and intellectual levels respectively.' This interested me deeply, and I tried to follow up this beginning by reading Alexander's *The Universal Constant In Living* when it appeared in 1941. But I found it an impossible book, ill-written, pretentious, and apparently more desirous of obscuring its subject than explaining it. Nevertheless, I did not think it was the work of a quack, but merely of an uncommonly clumsy writer.

As the years passed my curiosity continued unabated, and by 1955 I needed Alexander treatment badly, for I was worried by frequent and prolonged numbness in my left leg which had become so troublesome that at times it would make me stumble. A physician had examined it carefully, and could find nothing wrong, though he established to his own satisfaction that it was numb (which I had told him before) by sticking pins in it; his only proposal was that I might have an exploratory operation to see if I had a slipped disc, if the leg grew worse. Fortunately in November of this year I met a pupil of yours, and made arrangements to see you for lessons the following January.

Circumstances made it impossible for me to take lessons for the usual thirty days as I live at a considerable distance from New York, but as my wife was also keenly interested we came to you together, and you undertook to teach us in successive half-hours, so that while one was being instructed, the other watched. I do not think that you were confident that so short a period of lessons as we took that first time could do us much good, but it did. By the end of a week my left leg was much more comfortable, and we went away determined to continue working at home on the lines established by you.

Since that time we have visited you every six months. Between visits to you we have worked by ourselves, usually twice a day and missing, I think, no more than ten days in thirty months.

The results are of a kind difficult to describe, but fully bearing out Huxley's second statement, that 'such physical self-awareness and self-control leads to, and to some extent is actually a form of, mental and moral self-awareness and self-control.' This sounds like tall talk, but in actual experience it is not so.

To be specific, the trouble in my left leg disappeared and has only returned on two or three occasions when I was particularly tired, and then yielded at once to some Alexander work. Apart from this I have had a marked increase in physical well-being, and have been free from the periods of exhaustion and nervous weariness which used to follow intense work. My work (which is that of a writer and editor) forces me to spend long hours—ten hours a day is by no means uncommon—sitting at a desk, writing or reading. Only those who have done it for twenty years know how physically wearisome and demanding such immobility can be; in fact, it is not immobility, but a routine of twists, fidgets and jumps caused by thwarted muscles and nerves. Nature quite often gives the physiques of farm-labourers to those who do sedentary work. I am such a person, and the inactivity which my work requires is bought at a dear price, which is exacted in the currency of numb legs, dyspepsia, backache, headache, ill-temper, misanthropy and a weariness of body which demands violent physical exercise which weariness of mind makes unendurably distasteful.

Lessons with you, and daily private practice along the lines you point out, has made a most welcome change in this physical misery. I still sit at a desk all day and part of the night, but I sit in quite a different way; walking, which is my favourite exercise, has taken on a new quality of pleasure; because I am not nervously exacerbated, I plan my work better, and actually get more work done with less trouble; my misanthropy has dropped to quite a low level for one engaged in a notoriously misanthropic profession.

I know that you discourage your pupils from talking about psychological changes which follow work on Alexander's lines, and I appreciate the fact that cranks and featherweight messiahs must be discouraged. Nevertheless, I must add that during thirty months of Alexander work I have found new powers of endurance which are not solely physical. Everybody in their forties is trying to get his second wind for the second and hardest lap in the race of life; some people find it one way and some another, and a sad number do not find it at all, and seem to shrivel as the years pass. Whether I have found it in the Alexander lessons and their application I cannot, with complete confidence, say, but certainly they pointed the way to a development for which I had hoped, but could not have reached, unaided. As you yourself have said, the work emphasizes and discloses what the pupil essentially *is*, and in my own case I regard it as a means of self-exploration, as well as a technique of physical re-training.

With every best wish, I am,

Yours sincerely,
R.D.

This final letter is from an athlete:

As you remember, when I first took lessons from you I was a junior in college. At that time athletically I was concentrating on skiing, but it was in track that the significance of the lessons was first demonstrated to me. Previous years I had been out or track and had run the one-hundred-yard dash but never faster than 10.7 seconds. The spring of my Junior year I did not go out for track and I did no training. Rather than doing the usual exercises I worked on the head, neck and back pattern. I went into an intramural meet and the first day qualified for the finals. The next day, encountering none of the usual second-day stiffness common with those who are out of training, I returned a time 0.3 of a second faster than I had ever done.

This point is constantly being brought home to me that exercise serves only to reinforce bad habit patterns if the HN & B pattern is beginning to disintegrate. Thus the athlete who trains and trains will see his efficiency and co-ordination decrease. He envies the 'natural athlete' with his apparent ease and success. It has been my experience in watching many athletes in this focus that the naturals and champions have a fine pattern, good use. This is particularly true in a physiologically complicated sport such as skiing or tennis. Specific co-ordinations may be developed in such sports as distance running where a habit can become established and take over. These men pay the price in erratic and rapidly slipping performance while increased training only speeds up the disintegration.

Athletic coaching normally assumes good co-ordination as a prerequisite and then goes on and applies its theories. The exciting part of the Alexander Technique is that it deals directly with the total pattern of co-ordination. The athlete, then, with a higher level of general co-ordination, confronts the problems the sport presents. He is basically better equipped and is therefore capable of reaching a higher level of proficiency. Co-ordination is not such a fixed or settled thing as is believed; a lot can be done about it.

Athletes tend to think in terms of specific motions and lose sight of this total pattern which conditions the individual part moving to an extent of ten feet or three seconds, and makes the difference between a mediocre and a fine performance.

I certainly can go on about this subject; being here in training camp winds one up on these problems. Before coming here to train with the Italian National team I went to Switzerland and starting from the beginning tried to relearn the art of skiing. I have made some progress, but it is a tremendous task to relearn something so established and so complicated. One must make so many rapid decisions and adjustments. I had always envied the natural athlete his apparent ease and success, and now I begin to understand how the head, neck and back pattern make action easier and more efficient.

The ability to come back to a 'balanced resting state' (Barlow)—that is, one where the HN & B pattern is operating between moments of encountering the stress situation—is essential to the athlete. This has been particularly helpful to me in handling the anxiety states that an athlete in a dangerous and competitive sport must learn to cope with.

J.B.

Part Two

Alexander's discoveries

Chapter 12

ALEXANDER'S DISCOVERY OF THE HN & B PATTERN

Now we come to the story of Alexander's search and final achievement. It is a tale of adventure and hardship, one that calls forth great qualities of character and intellect and that ends in an achievement far greater than the goal originally sought.

I have often been asked: 'What led Alexander to make the search that resulted in his discovery?' 'How did it all start?' The immediate reason for his search was that he commenced having trouble with his voice, and as he was a professional reciter this was a serious matter. In describing how he first became interested in reciting, he said that as a boy he was delicate and had frequent bouts of illness that kept him at home, and so he started to read. Almost from the beginning his interest focused on the plays of Shakespeare. From then on he wanted to be a reciter, hoping that in time this would lead to him becoming a Shakespearean actor. Once the lure of the theatre has entered a man's blood, there is literally no exertion that seems too great, no task that seems too hard. So we can understand why he was willing to undertake so difficult a search and the powerful drive that sustained him in all its difficulties.

Alexander had been a successful reciter in Australia for a number of years, but in 1892 trouble arose. When he recited, he became increasingly hoarse and could be heard gasping and sucking in air through his mouth. (These were by no means unusual troubles either in his day or at the present time. One has only to turn on the radio to hear this gasping while listening to some of our best speakers, as well as some of our very good singers. In fact, the absence of it is uncommon. Hoarseness among those who use their voices professionally is also a very frequent problem.)

Alexander went to a throat specialist who diagnosed his trouble as irritation of the mucous membrane of the nose and throat and inflammation of the vocal cords. The doctor treated him in the customary way, with inhalations. Alexander continued going to throat specialists for a long time, but the gasping became more marked and the hoarseness recurred at shorter intervals and sometimes was so severe that it would result in his losing his voice entirely. He was greatly discouraged and apprehensive as to whether he would be able to continue in his career. Finally something happened which brought matters to a head. Alexander was offered an engagement—the most important one he had had so far. He was uncertain about accepting it and consulted his doctor once again.

The doctor told him that if he used his voice as little as possible during the two weeks before the engagement and did not recite at all, he could safely count on getting through his engagement. This remark of the specialist's started Alexander thinking: the man was implying that something harmful happened when he *used* his voice, particularly when he used it vigorously as he did in reciting.

Alexander acted on the doctor's advice and used his voice as sparingly as he could. Soon he began to feel hopeful, for his symptoms were disappearing. The night of the recital he was completely free from hoarseness. No sooner did he begin to use his voice, however, than his trouble started to come back. Halfway through the programme his voice was in very bad condition, and by the end of the evening he could hardly speak. He was much upset by what had happened, as his career was both his livelihood and his greatest interest, and it looked as if he would have to give it up.

Again he went to see his doctor and talked the matter over with him. Alexander pointed out that what had happened at the recital seemed to show that the trouble was caused by something he did when he used his voice. His voice was all right when he started the recital; but during the recital it went wrong. It was while he was using his voice that the change from right to wrong occurred. Alexander told us that when he had finished saying this, the doctor thought for a moment, and then said, 'Yes, that must be so.'

'Can you tell me what it is I do that causes the trouble?' Alexander asked. The doctor said that he could not. It was then that Alexander decided that he would have to study and experiment and find out for himself. His search began.

Up to this point Alexander had done what anyone else would do—he had gone to doctors and followed their advice. But from this point on he went his own individual way. From the moment he started his search we get one indication after another that his outlook was very different from other men's. The conclusion that his trouble was caused by something he did when he used his voice was a simple and logical one. The doctor had agreed that it must be so. Yet, how many people would have reached this conclusion, in the first place, or, having reached it, would have been willing to start a prolonged and arduous search to find out what the something was? Most of us tend to accept what the expert, the accepted authority on a subject, says; and if he has nothing to offer us, we let the matter rest. Not Alexander, however. Dr Ernest Jones, in discussing the conditions governing the productivity of genius (in *The Saturday Review*, August 10th, 1947) says:

> It has long struck me that an essential prerequisite of such productivity must be in a particular scepticism on the part of the genius. He must refuse to acquiesce in previously accepted conclusions. This argues a kind of *imperviousness to the opinion of others, notably of authorities*. Furthermore he has the capacity for *seeing the existence of a problem where others have passed it by; he has refused to take something for granted as being either without meaning or too insignificant to bother about*. This aloofness sets him free to speculate and investigate.

These words are peculiarly applicable to Alexander. The doctor's opinion and limitations did not influence him in the least. If something that he did with himself while reciting was the cause of his trouble, he was going to find out for himself what this was. His use of the body in reciting had become for him a problem of the greatest significance.

As we learn about the start of his research and contrast his subject, equipment and procedure with that of other research projects we know about, it is at first hard for us to fully grasp either his achievement or its importance. Our thoughts are too shackled by the familiar.

To do research we think one must have a grant from a foundation, a well-equipped modern laboratory, scientifically trained assistants—but as Dr Hans Selye points out, 'There are two ways of detecting something that nobody can see; one is to aim at the finest detail by getting as close as possible with the best available instruments; *the other is merely to look at things from a new angle where they show hitherto unexposed facets.*'* It was this latter way that Alexander followed. He had what Selye said were the necessary ingredients in his own search, an unbiased state of mind and a fresh point of view.

Alexander's problem, when expressed, sounds misleadingly simple. It was to find out what he did when he used his voice in reciting that was causing his trouble. This involved observing movement and co-ordination, and he was singularly well equipped to work on such a problem. His youth had been spent in Tasmania where he lived a simple frontier life with frontier people, problems, and interests. Men walked great distances, cut down trees, chopped wood. They had to handle themselves in such a way that they would have the least fatigue and greatest power; they selected stock and horses. A favourite sport was horse racing and everyone bet on these races. As they were vital problems to him, each man thought about co-ordination and movement both in men and in animals; his eyes were trained to see things that our eyes completely overlook. There was another useful side to this frontier life: it made for self-reliance and resourcefulness. These qualities were highly necessary to Alexander in his search, as in this he was alone, rudderless, and here was no existing knowledge to which he could turn. But to a frontiersman, such a situation presented nothing unusual. In frontier life if a man had a problem, there was no 'expert' at hand. He had to rely on himself

---
* *The Stress of Life*, McGraw-Hill, p. 37.

and handle the problem himself, with no aids beyond his own mind and body. It was quite literally a 'do-it-yourself' civilization. In the training course, Alexander often used the Greek word 'nous'. I believe the word actually means 'mind' or 'intellect', but he never used it in a way that would indicate that. He used it as if it means 'self-resourcefulness' and an ability of the mind to use knowledge. He would shake his head and say, 'People, today, have no nous', and when we asked him what he meant, he would say, 'They can't do anything for themselves; they can't work anything out.' It was strange to him to be in a country and civilization where self-resourcefulness was not taken for granted.

I have often been asked, when talking about his discovery, if he knew anatomy. He knew no anatomy except what he had observed and what he may have picked up in elocution lessons.

However, knowledge of this sort would not have helped him, as at the time he made his search his findings had no link with *any existing knowledge*. Much later on his discovery was linked up with the work of the physiologist Rudolf Magnus and the biologist G. E. Coghill, but at this time they had not been heard of, and Alexander's discovery was based solely on his own observations and experiments.

Alexander himself believed, and we agreed with him, that a knowledge of anatomy, far from aiding his discovery, would, in all likelihood, have prevented it. He would have been far less able to do what William James calls 'perceiving in an unhabitual way'.

Anatomical knowledge may well have affected adversely the manner in which he observed, in that it would have tempted him to have a slant and to try to synthesize what he saw and what he knew. As it was, he brought to his search an unprejudiced mind and a keen eye.

He began his search by observing himself in the mirror both when he was speaking and when he was reciting. At first he could detect nothing when he was speaking, but he noticed that when he was reciting he tended to do three things: to pull his head back, to depress his larynx, and to suck in air through his mouth in such a way as to produce a gasping sound. After making these observations, he went back and watched himself speaking, and he then noticed that here, too, he did the same three things, though to what seemed to him an infinitesimal degree. He again watched himself reciting and observed that the three tendencies became more marked when he used his voice forcefully and vigorously. These three things seemed to indicate some progress, in that he at least now knew what he did with himself when he used his voice, but for long months he could get no further. Since he did not know which of these three factors caused the other two, he proceeded to experiment with each of the three alternatives to discover whether any one of them caused either or both of the other two. For months he tried to stop the sucking in of breath when he recited and found he could not do so. He also tried not to depress the larynx when he recited and found he could not control this either. He was much surprised, for he had fully expected to be able to control these separate symptoms directly. He now tried not to pull his head back when he recited and found that not only was he able to control his head, but, greatly to his excitement, the action of his head controlled indirectly his breathing and the functioning of his larynx. This was the first landmark in Alexander's search: his dawning realization that the pulling back of the head was of great importance, because it caused other harmful symptoms.

Let us consider for a moment the procedure he used. He looked in the mirror and saw certain concrete things happening. They were tiny manifestations only, but they were quite concrete. He was not engaged in speculation, but in observing what actually happened. His method was objective throughout. He was concerned not with what he *felt* that he was doing with himself (quite the contrary, as we shall see later on), but with what he *saw* that he was doing with himself. He continued to experiment with the facts that he observed until bit by bit a relationship of cause and effect was established between them: the pulling back of the head caused the sucking in of breath and the depressing of the larynx. This same careful, painstaking objective method continued throughout his search. Now he had reached his first landmark: the importance of the head in conditioning for good or ill other parts of the body.

For practical reasons, man has always known that with steers and horses the position of the head greatly influences the body: that a steer, for example, can be thrown by a twist of the head; that the gait of a horse is greatly influenced by a check-rein; that draught horses required to pull heavy loads cannot function properly if their heads are held back with the check-reins. At a later date there were two extremely important conclusions based on laboratory experiments on animals, both strangely analogous to Alexander in that they corroborated his conclusion of the basic importance of the head.

The physiologist Rudolf Magnus of Utrecht, in his Edinburgh lectures (May 19-20, 1926) on the physiology of posture, points out that the mechanism of the body acts in such a way that the head leads and the body follows. Also, the biologist G. E. Coghill,* in his study on the development of the nervous system of the amblystoma, found that all movement proceeded from the head downward and that it never obtained complete autonomy from the head.

Alexander now continued his observations of the head while reciting. At first, he observed only his head and vocal organs. He experimented with putting his head forward, but he found that after a certain point was reached he tended to pull his head down as well as forward, and both his vocal and respiratory organs reacted to this precisely as though he were pulling his head back and down. His head, therefore, must go forward but not down. Again he continued watching himself in the mirror as he recited, but this time he observed his torso as well as his head and vocal organs. After more long, patient observations he was able to add something of great importance to his previous findings. The pulling back of the head was always accompanied by a tendency to lift the

---

* In his book *Anatomy and the Problem of Behaviour* (1929), Cambridge University Press.

chest which brought about a *narrowing* of the back and by a *shortening* of the stature which was caused by an exaggerated hollowing of the lower back. The torso had now come into the picture.

This was the second landmark in his search: the discovery that organs of speech were influenced *not by the head alone but by a connecting pattern between the head and torso*. He now started a series of experiments. In the first, he tried to prevent a shortening of his stature. In the second, he tried actually to lengthen his stature. He alternated between these two forms of experiment and found that the best functioning of his voice came when he lengthened his stature. However, to lengthen his stature he found that his head must go forward and up; when it went back and down or forward and down, his stature was shortened. He also added the widening of the back to the new pattern, because the pulling back of the head and the narrowing of the back always accompanied each other and were part and parcel of his old habit of using himself wrongly.

His findings now indicated that the head's going forward and up and the back's lengthening and widening would bring about the best conditions in which to use his voice. He had now worked out a definite relationship of the head, neck* and back, and was receiving proof that his specific voice troubles were disappearing in direct proportion to his establishing this relationship and maintaining it as he used his voice.

The first part of his search was ended. He had found he could not handle his voice trouble specifically, but that he could control it through a certain dynamic pattern of the head, neck and back. He could establish and strengthen this pattern when he was not speaking, and even this greatly lessened his voice difficulties, but he had not yet full control. It

---

* The neck is also included in the pattern. This is one of the important elements that Alexander left out in the story of his search in *The Use of the Self*. This omission will be discussed in Chapter 13, page 134.

was well-nigh impossible for him to *maintain* the pattern when he was reciting.

It was to this problem that he now turned his attention.

Before continuing with Alexander's research, however, it is important that the reader have a more detailed explanation of the HN & B relationship.

Chapter 13

DETAILED DISCUSSION OF THE HEAD, NECK AND BACK RELATIONSHIP

The head, neck and back relationship in order to be understood must be described and discussed in much more detail. There were many things that Alexander left out when he was writing about it, other things that he stated ambiguously. One had to fill in these gaps as best one could by talking to him and asking questions. Yet until one became fairly knowledgeable about his work, one really did not know what questions to ask. So that it was a long and hard process to form a clear, coherent idea of what, precisely, his work was, and of how one could achieve increasing mastery of it. It was extremely difficult, in short, to have all the pieces of the puzzle fit together and make an intelligible whole.

One of the first things that needs to be made clear is that Alexander's head, neck and back pattern was brought into operation by thought. At some time during the evolution of his technique he made the momentous change from 'doing' to 'thinking'. Originally, he wrote of 'putting' the head forward and up. Later, in his teaching and in his book he speaks of 'directing' or 'ordering' the head forward and up. He uses the words 'directing' and 'ordering' synonymously with 'thinking'. It took some time, though, for his students to find this out, for he never told us directly. Nor did he ever give us a verbal account of the change from 'doing' to 'thinking'. He touches on it, however, in his books. In *Man's Supreme Inheritance** (page 203), he says:

> He [the pupil] must learn to give the correct mental orders to the mechanisms involved, and *there must be a clear differentiation in his mind between the giving of the order and the performance of the act ordered and carried out through the medium of the muscles.*†

---

* E. P. Dutton. † Italics are Alexander's.

The Head, Neck and Back Relationship

He then goes on to say that the pupil's order must be merely a framing and holding of a desire in his mind and not the physical performance of an act and that if the pupil does this last he will invariably fail.

Here he at least makes the distinction between 'thinking' (or ordering) and 'doing' and tells us that 'doing' will always fail. So that at least we have the reason for the change from 'doing' to 'thinking'. Every pupil tries to 'do' at first, and finds that it doesn't work. Dr Ian Stevenson, in some notes on Alexander's work, says:

> The reason for this is that muscular activities, being governed by proprioceptive stimuli, will be incorrect if these stimuli are incorrect, or incorrectly interpreted as they are in most people. The majority of persons when they try to move their heads forward and up, either move them forward and down or upward and back, but not forward and up. They simply do not have that much conscious control of their head and neck muscles.
>
> Most people know when they strike a wrong note on the piano, because they have sensory training to deal with auditory stimuli. They do not have sensory training to deal with their own muscular stimuli.

The only indirect mention that I can call to mind that Alexander ever made to us of the necessity of getting the head, neck and back pattern into operation by 'thinking' instead of by 'doing' was when he quoted a remark that John Dewey had once made to him: 'Was it not wonderful, Alexander, that you came across the idea of non-doing in doing concrete things?'

Another crucially important event that Alexander never mentioned or wrote about was his decision that thinking the neck free must be the first step—the initial step—in the process of setting the new head, neck and back pattern to work. Nor did he ever say what led him to this decision. The idea of thinking the neck free is extremely baffling to the pupil, and understandably so, because he finds that the neck is not freed simply by virtue of his thinking it free. It does, however, become freer; the head thus has a chance to tend to go forward

Fig. 16. This Egyptian figure illustrates the integration of the pelvis with the back rather than with the legs. A pupil of mine, seeing this photograph, said, 'Is not that back rather exaggeratedly straight and "all of a piece".' 'Very little, if any,' I said, 'there is as you see a slight curve in the lower spine. Your wife has good control and she is about to sit down with the new pattern working. If she is successful doing this notice her back.' This wife was successful and the pupil ran his hand over her back. 'Why, it's like a billiard table,' he said. Alexander often quoted a description that one of the Rowntrees gave of his work. It was this: 'Reasoning from the known to the unknown, *the known being wrong* and the *unknown right.*' In this field the unfamiliar-looking back is not necessarily an ill-functioning back, just the opposite is likely to be true. (Statue of King Seusert I, XII Dynasty, c. 1950 BC).

in relation to it, and the right process can start. The real freedom of the neck is dependent upon the alignment and functioning of the back. But once the right process has started, the back will improve steadily, and with this improvement the complete freedom of the neck can be progressively attained. To think the neck free, therefore, is to set in motion a beneficent circle.

So far we know that to get the head, neck and back pattern operating the Alexander pupil must first think the neck free, then think the head forward and up. The words 'head forward' call for explanation. Alexander both said and wrote simply 'head forward' and this has led to a great deal of confusion as well as some completely wrong impressions. 'Head forward' might have several meanings. Most people think of it as head forward in space. Alexander in using the words meant head forward in relation to the neck. It took a long time and hard work to find this out. One realized in time that his hands, which he used in demonstrating and teaching, were always tending to take the neck back and the head forward in relation to it. Once one had discovered this, one could ask him a direct question and get his confirmation that 'head forward' meant 'head forward in relation to the neck'. The head's tending to go forward in relation to the neck causes the alignment of the head and neck to improve, in that the head is balanced on top of the neck instead of being retracted back upon it. Once this retraction or locking is done away with, the head will tend to go up whether any other thought is given or not, just as the plant will come up out of the ground if it is not prevented or interfered with. If in addition the head is thought up, however, it will go up more strongly.

The majority of doctors and most of the general public in using the phrase 'head forward' mean head forward in space. There is widespread misunderstanding about Alexander's use of the phrase and also some downright erroneous ideas about it.

A New York doctor once said to me, 'The trouble is that Alexander is anatomically wrong.' As we talked it out, I discovered that she thought—and naturally enough—that 'head forward' meant 'head forward in space'.

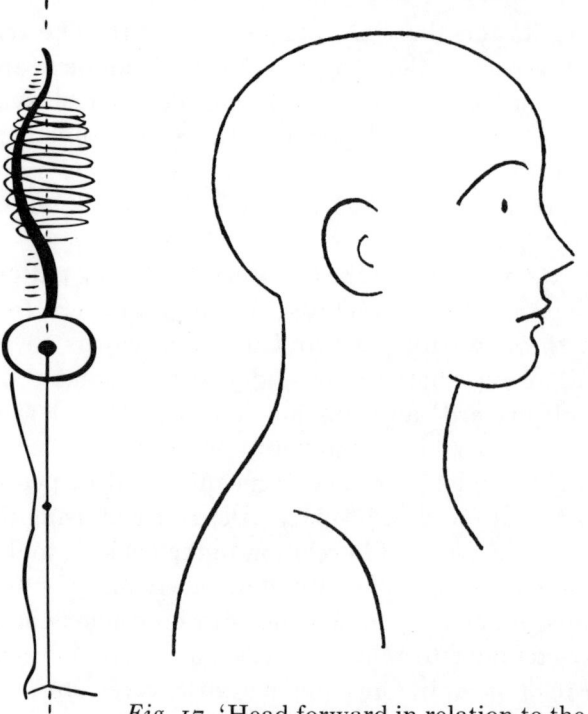

Fig. 17. 'Head forward in relation to the neck.'

I am reproducing here two drawings by George Hughes. They indicate (fig. 17) the normal carriage of the head, and (fig. 18) a faulty posture which places the centre of gravity of the head too far forward.

Figure 17 most nearly approximates Alexander's 'head forward' or, as we shall now say, 'head forward in relation to the neck'. In looking at figures 17 and 18 one may be helped visually to understand why 'head forward in relation to the neck' unlocks the head on the neck. In figure 17 the head is foursquare on the neck—in line with the neck, as it were, and on top of it. There is no interference with its going up. In figure 18 the head is not in line with the neck. It is in front of it, and at the place where the two join, the head is pulled back and there is a locking. One sees here the interdependency of the head and neck in the 'forward' step. The neck will gradually tend to go back as the head tends to go forward in relation to it.

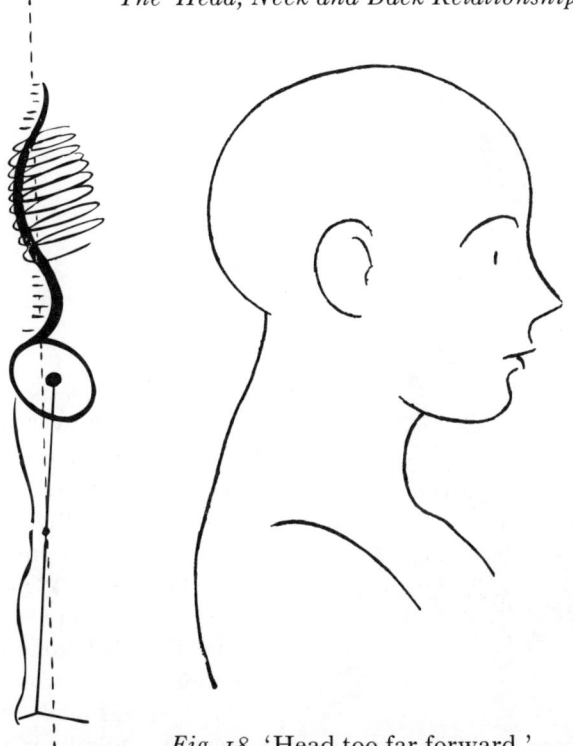

Fig. 18. 'Head too far forward.'

It is important to get these semantic difficulties and misunderstandings cleared up. Otherwise many people, and the medical profession in particular, will take Alexander's use of the phrase 'head forward' to mean the exact opposite of what he intended it to mean.

To return to Alexander's head, neck and back relationship: the pupil now knows that to get this pattern operating he must first think the neck free, then the head forward in relation to the neck and up. We can now discuss the final parts of the pattern, the lengthening and widening of the back. But before we begin to consider the back by itself, let us realize that we can never possibly consider the back by itself. We can never, as it were, get rid of the head, because what the head does conditions and determines what the back does. If the head goes back and down, the back will shorten and narrow. If the head goes forward and up, the back will lengthen and widen, even if no further thought is given to the process. But if no

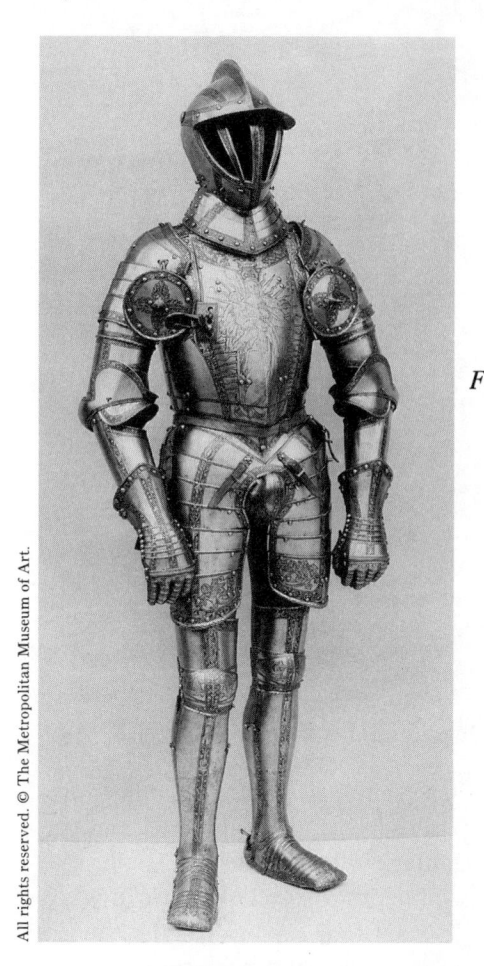

Fig. 19. This figure is included to show how the arms are placed in the sockets when the pattern is working and the back lengthening and widening. As you look at this figure note that the backs of the hands are facing you. Armour was made for active men who needed skill in handling themselves. (German suit of parade armour made for Albrecht v, Duke of Bavaria, 1549.)

thought is given, the process of lengthening and widening will be weak. To have strength, we must give additional thoughts to the back (after we have given them to the head and neck). One never gives isolated thoughts to the back alone; the pattern brings together the various steps in a sequence, each step being dependent on the preceding step.

One thing that it is important for us to realize in considering the thoughts given to the back is that the back includes the pelvis; it does not stop at the waistline. And what Alexander meant by 'lengthening the back' is that one must think the whole back, including the pelvis, upwards.*

---
* F. M. Alexander, in conversation with the author.

Fig. 20. This figure in armour shows the extraordinary grace in walking or taking a single step when the pattern is leading and the movement of the leg is conditioned by the pattern and is subordinate to it. Contrast this with newspaper photographs of politicans walking (it seems to be most often politicians who are caught in this act!). Here you will see the leg leading and dragging the body out of alignment. The back will appear to be working in two or more sections. (Italian Gothic suit of armour, c. 1480).

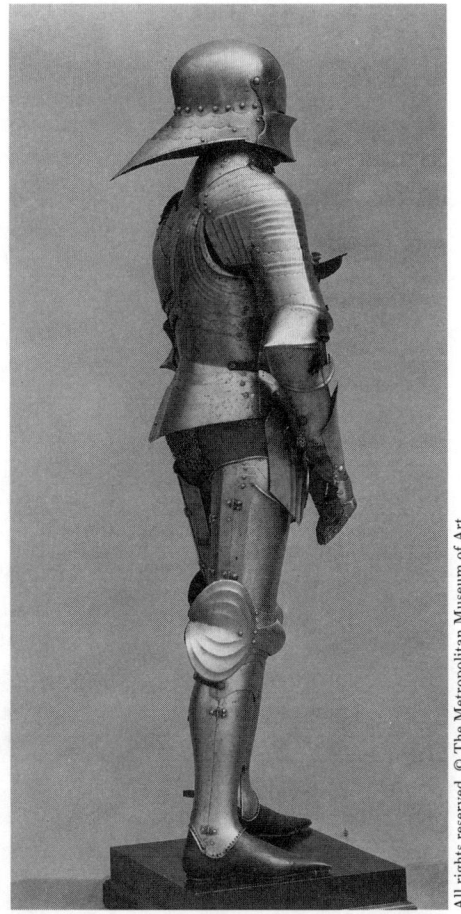

The words 'to think the whole back upwards' may have little meaning or importance for the average reader; but for those who, through having had the correct experience, are equipped to give such thoughts or orders, they are a very present help in time of practical difficulty.

I remember an instance in which a young pianist who was having serious difficulties with his technique began thinking 'the whole back upwards' as he played. Previously, he had split the back into two sections, making a false joint in the lumbar spine. (This is a very common fault in pianists. Even a layman can observe the great mobility in the upper back of a pianist and the frozen immobility of the lower back.) And directly he stopped using his back as though the upper and lower parts of it were unrelated, there was a vast improvement in his playing. He could get over the keyboard with much greater ease and flexibility, his tone was much better, and the follow-through of his tone was less clipped. When the back does not fulfil its proper function, the arms are obliged to take on more than their proper function. Of necessity they develop strains, and this affects the tone and power of the pianist.

The last step in the pattern is the widening of the back. This may be a little difficult for the reader to comprehend; for many people have been taught that lengthening the back by itself is a good thing and alleviates a variety of ills: lengthening at any price—straining, shoving, pulling the guts up, hanging from a halter rigged up in the clothes closet! A few readers may think that widening, by itself, is a good thing, as it sometimes relieves specific pains. But really to comprehend the idea of lengthening and widening, one must be given the experience. The experience is necessary, yet word pictures, by clearing away some of the intellectual difficulties in the way of understanding, can make it easier for the reader to attain the experience. Think of a towel that is pulled taut vertically but not horizontally. The towel is probably much narrower than it is normally, as it may have folds or ridges vertically. Something of the same sort happens in a human body. When a back is lengthening but not widened, a narrowing takes place and the back of the rib cage will be curved inward. There will be a groove in the middle of the back where the spine is, and the shoulder-blades will be close together and unduly prominent. In movement, all these tendencies are even more pronounced. If you will just put your hand on the back of the person in question, you will feel when he moves that his spine is tending to go away from your hand and to form a deeper groove. The shoulder-blades come even closer together, and the back of the rib cage curves inwards increasingly. Let us now think of a towel that is pulled taut both vertically and horizontally, as a painter's canvas is, on a frame. This would correspond to a back that is lengthening

The Head, Neck and Back Relationship 143

Fig. 21. This figure illustrates the kind of knee thrust a man has if the pattern is working. Note the strength and significance of this knee thrust. Most often the bent knees that we see today are weak and wobbly looking. (Etruscan Warrior, in style of 5th century BC.)

and widening. This is by no means a perfect analogy, as with a back there is always a dynamic quality, but it may help. In a lengthening and widening back, the shoulder-blades tend to go apart, the measurement of the back of the rib cage to increase, and the groove in the middle of the back to become smaller.

The analogy of the towel, imperfect as it is, will serve, I think, to emphasize my point that the pattern Alexander discovered cannot be understood as a number of separate pulls or adjustments. It consists, rather, of contrary adjustments ('head forward and up', 'back lengthening and widening'), which meet together and produce co-ordination. It might also help the reader if he would think of what is involved in putting up a tent. A tent cannot be erected by driving one stake. There must be several stakes, all of which, attached to ropes and taken together, set up the series of contrary pulls which are necessary if the tent is to stand and fulfil its function. It is much the same way with the human body. The whole pattern can now be stated thus: the pupil is to think the neck free, the head forward (in relation to the neck) and up, the back lengthening and widening.

This chapter was written to fill in the gaps that Alexander left when he wrote of his research, so that the head, neck and back pattern he discovered might be intellectually comprehensible to the reader. It was not written in the belief that anyone can teach himself Alexander's work. Personally, I have never met a person who has been able to learn this way. I have met a number of people who have claimed to have learned this way, but when they were examined it was found that they had not done so.

For a person who is attempting to learn Alexander's work from written or verbal instructions, there are pitfalls at every turn. Alexander himself never learned through words. He learned through a series of experiences. So the pupil, to learn, must be given the experience again and again, so that the experience and the appropriate words will be associated in the pupil's consciousness. The general semanticists say, very properly, that words are *maps* of a certain territory, but they are not the territory itself. When one considers the truth of this, one will readily see that there are many things which cannot be learned, much less made a part of one's mind and body, through words alone.

The Head, Neck and Back Relationship

Fig 22. This figure is an example of what we do not want; a forward neck, a head retracted back upon it and a shortened overwide back. This is an example of some of the deformities the body can get into when the pattern is not working. (Greek marble portrait of an unidentified man, Hellenistic Period).

Chapter 14

OTHER DISCOVERIES OF ALEXANDER'S

In Alexander's struggles to maintain the new HN & B pattern when he was reciting, certain other facts of the greatest importance were brought to light.

The first of these facts was that feeling is untrustworthy.*

When Alexander began his experiments, he used, as we will remember, a mirror. When he first tried to apply the new pattern to his reciting, however, he was not using a mirror. He thought that he was maintaining the new pattern; he *felt* that he was maintaining the new pattern; but the difficulties with his voice returned. This made him suspect that he was not doing what he thought or felt he was doing. He therefore decided to check, and using three mirrors (placing the outer two at different angles to the middle one so that he could get several different views of himself), he was enabled to see that at the moment when he was about to speak he put his head not forward, as he had intended, but back. He was doing the opposite of what he had believed and felt he was doing.

Now, for the first time, he asked himself whether he had any definite guiding principle for determining the way he used himself; he could only answer that he had none. He simply used himself in the way that *felt* right and natural to him. His *feeling* was his only guide, and now he knew that his feeling was unreliable.

Alexander tells us, in *The Use of the Self*, page 21, that he was deeply discouraged at this point. But he showed his usual dogged determination to find a way out. 'Surely,' he argued, 'if it is possible for feeling to become untrustworthy as a means

---

* 'Feeling', as the word is used here, has nothing to do with local or cutaneous sensation, but applies to sensory nerves that serve the muscles, the tendons, the joints, and the middle ear. This is in essence Coghill's explanation of the term 'proprioceptive'.

of direction, it should also be possible to make it trustworthy again.'

He had not all the pieces of the puzzle in his grasp as yet, but he had this flash of insight—perhaps feeling could become reliable again if the use of his body became right again. He was making a connection between his faulty HN & B pattern and the unreliability of his feeling, and his surmise proved to be correct—so much so that his work is often called *sensory re-education*, for when a person acquires this new pattern his feelings become increasingly reliable.

Alexander had assumed that the wrong way in which he used himself was his own personal disability. Now when he discovered the unreliability of his feelings, he decided to test and observe other people that he might the better appraise and corroborate his discoveries about himself. For the first time he included other people in his research. He tested both their HN & B patterns and the reliability of their feelings, and to his great surprise he found that both were faulty in the same way his own had been.

The extent of his findings had been greatly enlarged. His research was no longer an individual affair but included the habits and reactions of other people.

All these things had come to light in his attempts to solve the crucial problem which he had not yet solved: namely that of maintaining the new HN & B pattern in the acts of speaking and reciting. Alexander now continued observing himself in mirrors to try to find a clue as to this last problem. He tells us that he persevered, for months, without enlightenment. (Note the patience and determined perseverance of the man!) Finally, one day a light dawned, not the light he had hoped for, as his final problem was still unsolved, but another vital discovery was made. His observations had finally shown him that *it was not just his vocal organs he was using incorrectly when he recited; it was other parts of his body as well.* He used his hands and arms in reciting to make gestures; he used his feet and legs to stand and walk. In all these parts there was an exaggerated amount of tension and muscular imbalance. In short, there was a combined wrong use of his whole organism.

The scope of his original discovery of the HN & B pattern was now completely changed. It would help not merely those who had voice trouble, but everyone who was using himself wrongly, and in our civilization that meant almost everyone. At the culmination of his search Alexander tested out this hypothesis continually and found that it held—the operation of the new HN & B pattern would affect wrong use and functioning on other parts of the body just as it had, in the first instance, affected his own vocal and respiratory organs.

At this point in his research, and even before he had the corroboration of his teaching experience, Alexander suspected that the specific troubles that so many people had in different parts of their bodies were due to their faulty HN & B patterns. One has only to look at a group of ordinary people gathered in any room to see the distortions, deformities, and malfunctioning that exists in almost everyone, and Alexander's conclusion was that the great majority of people in our civilization had gone wrong: they had gone wrong in the way they used their bodies.

In formulating what he believed to be the reasons for man's going wrong in this way, Alexander, for the first time, reasoned theoretically. Until now, no theory had entered into his search: he had observed concrete things, drawn logical deductions from these things, and experimentally proved these deductions. It is a most plausible theory that he evolved, but the reader should keep in mind that it is a theory and therefore in a different category from his previous work.

Alexander concluded that man's direction of himself, based as it was on nothing but feeling, was as unreasoning and instinctive as the direction of animals. He believed that in our civilization, which calls for continuous and rapid adaptation to an ever-changing environment, such unreasoned, instinctive direction of use is no longer adequate and should be supplanted by a conscious rational principle.

One day in the training course he gave us an example illustrating his theory. A city cat, he said, is used to a complex environment and is seldom run over, but dodges in and out of traffic in the most able way. A country cat, brought to the city, is almost always run over. The sudden change from a simple to a complex environment is too much for the cat's instinctive powers of adaptation.

Alexander also said that people sometimes thought they were adopting a conscious principle when they controlled consciously specific bodily movements, but he was speaking of a conscious principle of direction that would apply to the organism as a whole.

Later, when the universal bearing of Alexander's discoveries was recognized by those who had experienced his work, other theories were advanced as to why man had begun to use his body incorrectly and why his feelings had become unreliable. One doctor believed the incorrect usage to be the carry-over of a primitive instinct—an instinct valuable in man's early environments but harmful in his later one.* This doctor held that the biologically useful factor of fear had caused the ancestors of primitive man to crouch and to throw back their heads so that they could not be seen over shrubs and grasses by wild animals. Later, he held, as the genus *Homo sapiens* evolved, there was a carry-over from this early habit, and because of it man had never adapted himself completely to the erect position.

Dr Millard Smith, of Boston, believes that man went wrong because fundamentally he is a mammal. His position in the uterus causes him to be equipped for a four-legged position because all his flexor muscles are flexed during pregnancy and when he is born they are shortened (in contrast to the extensor muscles of the trunk and pelvis). When man stands erect he is under the continuous strain of shortened flexor muscles. This leads to a situation where the pelvis is held in a vice by these shortened muscles.†

The biologist G. E. Coghill, in his 'Appreciation', printed at the beginning of Alexander's book *The Universal Constant*

---

* 'Instinct and Functioning in Health and Disease', by Dr Peter Macdonald, *British Medical Journal*, December 25, 1926.
† This hypothesis links up very aptly with some of the problems the Alexander teacher meets, such as integrating the pelvis with the rest of the back.

in Living,* suggests that some of the institutions of our present civilization are responsible for putting man wrong. He considers the chair most harmful. The squatting position which we used to use requires extreme stretching of the extensor muscles of the legs and abduction of the thighs, while the constant use of the chair prevents this stretching of the extensor muscles and tends to produce adduction of the thighs.

There are also other theories concerning the factors in our present civilization which tend to throw us off. In the article by Alma Frank, 'A Study in Infant Development', there are some photographs of infants who have been *pulled up by someone's hands* into a sitting position and infants who have *brought themselves up* into a sitting position. The head, neck and back patterns of the infants in the two groups are strikingly different. In the first group the children's heads are invariably pulled forward and down; the backs are shortened, narrowed so much that the shoulder-blades are sticking out and are close together. In the second group the head is beautifully poised, erect on the neck. And the back has the appearance of an integrated unit, with no visible signs of compression or narrowing. The photographs tell their own story better and more strikingly than any words can do. The difference in the head, neck and back patterns of the two groups is clear to the eye of any layman.

There are so many factors that tend to throw a child off from the correct head, neck and back pattern, and to destroy his co-ordination, that no child is likely to escape them all. Only a few examples of them will be given here. When an adult walks with a child, for instance, he often takes the child's arm and pulls it up. This action can in itself be harmful to the integration of the child's back; but in addition to this, the child is forced to adapt his pace to that of the adult. He is forced to go too quickly, and to take steps that are too long for his height and co-ordination. Then, too, babies and small children are frequently handled by adults with very stiff hands, and this can cause them to stiffen unduly. Again,

---

* E. P. Dutton & Co.

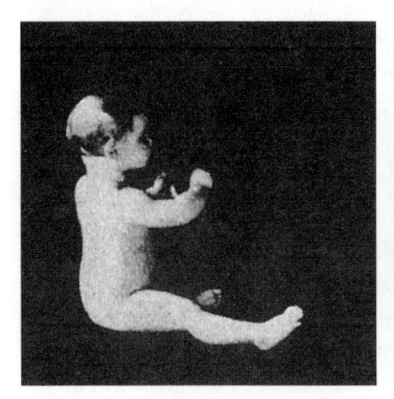

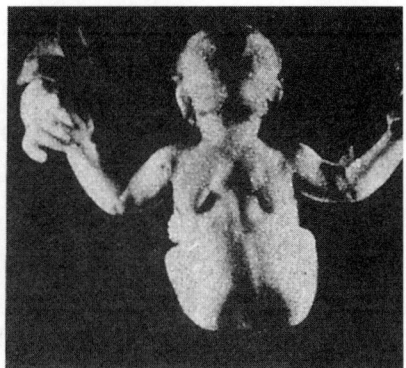

Fig. 23. Mary, 8 months. Sitting attained without adult aid, and sitting as pulled-to-sitting by adult. From Alma Frank, 'A Study in Infant Development' (*Child Development*, Vol. 9, No. 1, March 1938).

ambitious mothers often encourage their children to sit up before the bodily co-ordination necessary for this act has been fully developed. Finally, one of the most common—and certainly one of the most important—of the factors which influence both children and adults to go wrong is the psychological one; for the psychological tensions of our environment produce physiological tensions, in one degree or another, in the bodies of almost everyone.

But whatever may be the factor or the combination of factors that set men wrong originally, Alexander held that the way for men to right themselves again was to be more conscious of the way in which they used themselves, and to adhere, regardless of their feelings—one might almost say regardless of their sensory delusions—to a conscious, rationally worked out plan of procedure.

Chapter 15

ALEXANDER'S TECHNIQUE OF INHIBITION

In the introduction to Alexander's book, *Constructive Conscious Control of the Individual*,* John Dewey says in regard to inhibition: 'Mr Alexander has demonstrated a new scientific principle with respect to human behaviour as important as any principle which has ever been discovered in the domain of external nature.'

Alexander used the words *inhibit* and *inhibition* in *the physiological sense, not in the Freudian sense. The inhibitory is that function of the brain which says 'yes' or 'no' to the idea of a given activity.* 'Inhibition, as we do it,' he once said to his students, 'is not suppression but volition. It enables us to do what we have decided we want to do.'

Each one of us uses this inhibitory function of the mind and says 'yes' or 'no' to various activities all day long. I decide to leave the room, for example; my mind makes a decision and my body carries it out. Or, I may first decide to leave the room, and then I change my mind and decide not to leave it. The inhibitory function of my brain is at work—my body starts towards the door and then stops.

Alexander's inhibitory decisions were more clearly conscious than ours are apt to be in our everyday activities; that is the difference. The process is the same, and the same function of the brain is used.

It was the need to solve his final and most difficult problem that led him to develop his technique of inhibition. This problem was how to maintain the new HN & B pattern in speaking and reciting.

At what he called the 'critical moment'—that is the moment when he began to speak—he had never been able to control his reaction but would revert to his old faulty pattern.

He tried various ways of meeting this difficulty. First, he would strengthen the new pattern by repeating directions to

* E. P. Dutton & Co.

the head, neck and back many times. Then he tried refusing to respond immediately to the stimulus to speak. He argued that if we react immediately to a given stimulus, our response is bound to be our habitual one. It will be automatic and unconscious, and there will be small chance of controlling or changing it. Therefore, he said 'no' when the stimulus to speak came, and cut off any immediate reaction. This gave him a chance to act consciously. But neither of these methods solved his problem. He still could not control what he did at the 'critical moment'. At that moment he would always throw away the new HN & B pattern.

Alexander now asked himself, where did the trouble start? He went over very carefully in his mind what actually happened and decided that he had no control over what he did with his body once the *idea* of speaking had come into his head. It was the *idea* that caused the trouble and brought about a reversion to the old pattern in spite of all his intentions and desires. He then decided that *the idea of speaking and the body pattern he had always used when speaking must be inseparably fused*, and that to eliminate the old faulty pattern he would have to eliminate the idea of speaking. His problem was to get rid of the idea of speaking and yet speak! What a staggering feat of control lay before him! Most of us would have stopped then and there. Earlier in this book we were brought face to face with some of Alexander's weaknesses and limitations—but now we see the truly great qualities that he showed throughout his research, and particularly at this point where he met, perhaps, his hardest challenge.

In going over the bare narrative facts of Alexander's discovery it is easy to become absorbed in the discovery itself and to forget or pass over the qualities of mind and character that made such work possible. The greatest qualities he had were called up now: patience, logic, undauntedness in the face of seemingly impossible difficulties, creative ability to deduce certain hypotheses from the facts at hand, and extraordinary discipline in testing out and establishing these hypotheses. But his most impressive quality at this point, I think, was his undauntedness.

The first thing he decided on as a means of overcoming this impasse was to break up the act of speaking into its smallest steps, such as opening the mouth, making a sound, saying a word, etc. He would then focus his attention on each one of these separate steps in turn rather than on the idea of speaking. He tried a number of times to see if he could maintain the new HN & B pattern while he opened his mouth, then while he made a sound, and so forth.

Sometimes he was successful. He had almost solved his problem, but not quite, because the very act of opening his mouth or making a sound would tend to bring the idea of speaking into his mind. To counter this, he decided from the very beginning to say 'no' to the idea of speaking and renew this inhibitory decision constantly. When he did this, he was completely successful!

Alexander's technique of inhibition, therefore, consists of three elements: (1) a continually renewed decision to inhibit or say 'no' to the idea of speaking; (2) continually renewed thoughts to activate the new head, neck and back pattern; (3) the breaking down of the act of speaking into its smallest steps and the focusing on each step separately as if it were the end.

These three elements work together—there is a blend or intertwining between the three. It is this technique that successfully eliminated the idea of speaking and made it possible for Alexander to maintain the new HN & B pattern when he spoke and recited. With the new pattern operating, his vocal organs were used in an entirely different way and he was freed from his difficulties.

It was often extraordinarily difficult to say 'no' to the idea of speaking, since by opening his mouth, making a sound, etc., he was continually tempting himself to go wrong, so that sometimes he used auxiliary methods to help him focus his interest on the means or method and weaken his interest in the end or idea of speaking. He would, for example, go through his regular procedure and not speak at all but lift his arm instead, that is, *change his end*; he would also go through his procedure many times, thus *delaying his end*. Each of these methods made it easier for him to carry out successfully his basic inhibitory technique, in that they 'distracted' him from the idea of speaking and weakened his interest in it, while on the other hand they focused and strengthened his interest in the means that would enable him to speak in a new way.

In solving this problem of maintaining his new HN & B pattern in speaking, Alexander had evolved a new form of control. He called it 'control in process', or 'control throughout the process'. He said that when people spoke of control, they most often meant control by elimination, that is, the stimulus to go wrong is eliminated, as when a drunkard is sent to a sanatorium and all liquor is removed. But in the kind of control he developed, the stimulus to go wrong was always there, meeting you at every turn. He said it was as if you brought a drunkard into a room where there was whisky and said to him, 'Here, taste this, smell this, and then do whatever you have rationally decided you want to do about it.'

This is a form of control infinitely harder than any that we usually have to deal with. It may be objected that in the case of a drunkard the stimulus to go wrong would arouse powerful emotions and that he would be much harder pressed than a man tempted with the idea of speaking, it being assumed that the latter situation would be free of emotions.

Whatever the relative strength of the temptation to go wrong may be in these two instances, let no one assume that a man faced with overcoming a basic neuromuscular pattern of years' standing has not the power of emotion against him. There is unity, not separation, in a man's muscular and psychological patterns; they express man's adaptation to and often his defence against the outside world; and when a basic change comes, it is as if he gives up what he has known and is familiar with and steps out naked into an unknown country.

In the perfecting of his technique of inhibition, Alexander had worked out a means whereby man can, in dealing with his bodily habits, react as he has rationally decided he wishes to react, thus enabling him to free himself from the harmful habits of many years.

We are all of us frequently confronted with the problem of ends and mean. Does the end justify the means—and can one go after the end directly?

In working out his technique for the control and change of habit, Alexander found that unfailingly the means condition the end, and that no desired end can be attained directly, but only indirectly by adhering to rationally worked out means.

It was these findings of Alexander that Aldous Huxley considered of such paramount importance.

This ends the story of Alexander's nine long years of research. He started with one fact: that he used himself wrongly when he recited. His equipment was one mirror. He had no help, and his education was not extensive. Yet so extraordinary were his qualities of mind and character that, as Aldous Huxley says in the *Saturday Review of Literature*, October 25th, 1941, the man 'has come, by the oldest of indirect roads, to be a quite uniquely important, because uniquely practical, philosopher, educator, and physiologist.'

Chapter 16

Summary and evaluation

Alexander's own story answers the question as to why his work is not better known in the world today. He was a genius with great qualities and great limitations. Most often the very qualities that enabled him to make his discoveries hindered him in establishing his work.

Perhaps his most outstanding trait was his unrelatedness to others, and while this had been the greatest asset to him in the long isolation of his search, it was a serious obstacle to him in the task of establishing his work. He seemed unable to join with other people in any co-operative enterprise. He turned down in a somewhat indiscriminate way promising opportunities offered him that would have spread his work.

In handling concrete things Alexander had the greatest skill; in handling words he was most inept. Aldous Huxley points out in his book *Tomorrow and Tomorrow and Tomorrow*[*] how rarely is one man able to handle adequately both abstract ideas and concrete things. It is as if these two talents are in opposition to each other and cannot be united. Certainly Alexander bore out this thesis. The whole story of his search is a record of his observance of tiny concrete manifestations and his comprehension of their significance. It was this mastery of concrete things that enabled him to make his discovery of the head, neck and back pattern.

His unrivalled skill in using his hands as a teacher is another example of his skill with concrete things, and in this one instance the same talent aided both the spread of his work and the success of his search.

But on the other side of the picture, his weakness in handling words severely handicapped him in establishing his work. Often he was unable to get over to his pupils what his initial instructions actually meant. He would also make broad

---
* Harper & Row.

generalizations and startling statements intended to impress people, but most often he succeeded only in arousing their distrust. It was his somewhat loose way of speaking of the Primary Control, however, that was perhaps the most serious factor in causing distrust and alienating from him a group which could have been most valuable in helping to get his work on a more authoritative basis.

But apart from his qualities, how much of his creative energy did he put into the task of establishing his work? He wrote four books—a mighty labour indeed!—and enough to indicate that at certain periods in his life he had a deep interest in making his work better known. But we have the paradox that in all other projects designed to make his work better known and continuous after his lifetime his interest was tepid. He taught twenty-five years in London before starting to train teachers, and only then when he was under considerable pressure to do so. Frequently he was bored when training his student teachers. He was not interested in their professional progress or in their competency after graduation. His relationship to his students was always a personal rather than a professional one. He never seemed to look on them as having importance because the future of his work was in their hands.

In contrast to this lukewarmness, we have but to turn to the tremendous creative effort that he put into his dramatic activities, where every power he had was alert and active, and indeed he often seemed to transcend his own powers. It was his longing to be an actor that was the motive for his search and that gave him the strength to carry it through in the face of the greatest difficulties. Certainly his strongest emotional urge was directed towards acting.

We have every reason to be thankful that he possessed the emotional drive that he did and the particular combination of qualities that he did, for it was these which brought about his great achievement.

To complete Alexander's story we need to consider his outlook on knowledge and his own peculiarly individual way of pursuing knowledge.

He was often discouraged in his search but he never lacked confidence that he himself unaided would have the resources necessary to solve his problem. It was his own powers that he relied upon to an astonishing degree, not authority or tradition or the customary way of looking at things. He would often say to us in our student days, 'Never look for authority where authority is.'

He did not *ever* allow himself to get very far from the concrete. His conclusions were based on concrete happenings. He did not go far along the ladder of abstraction and have 'ideas about ideas'.

Finally and pre-eminently, for Alexander, knowledge, in order to be knowledge, must provide the solution of the problem. (One can imagine that this outlook must stem directly from his pioneer background. In a frontier civilization a man could not be said to know how to mend a roof unless he was able to stop the leaks.)

One of Alexander's favourite stories was of a group of anatomists who came to see him in his early days in London with a proposal that they study together. 'They were walking deformities,' Alexander said, imitating how each one looked as he came into the room. 'There is something terribly wrong here,' he added. It was inexplicable to him that their knowledge of anatomy did not enable them to prevent their own bodies from becoming deformed.

There are various ways of pursuing knowledge, ways that appear different and yet supplement each other. Be that as it may, Alexander's way—uniquely individual—was crowned with a success that fills those of us who are his followers with gratitude and awe.

It is my hope that this book, by clearing up the puzzlement that has surrounded Alexander's name and work, will cause an even larger audience to recognize him for what he was—a very great human benefactor. As to the unique benefits of his work, I think no one, perhaps, has given voice to these more comprehensively and appreciatively than Aldous Huxley.

Complete understanding of the system can only come with the practice of it. All I need say in this place is that I am sure, as a matter of personal experience and observation, that it gives us all the things we have been looking for in a system of physical education—relief from strain due to maladjustment and consequent improvement in physical and mental health; increased consciousness of the physical means employed to gain the end proposed by the will, and along with this a heightening of consciousness on all levels; technique of inhibition, working on the physical level to prevent the body from slipping back under the influence of greedy 'end-gaining' into the old habits of mal-co-ordination and working (by a kind of organic analogy) to inhibit undesirable impulses and irrelevancies on emotional and intellectual levels respectively. We cannot ask more for any system of physical education; nor if we seriously desire to alter human beings in a desirable way can we ask less.

Chapter on Education in *Ends and Means*, Harper & Row, 1937

Part Three

Appendixes

A. Clarification of Terms 1 and 2

1. When such terms as 'mind', 'body', physical' and 'psychological' are used in this book, their meaning and significance are to be understood in the light of the following quotations from Kurt Goldstein's book *The Organism*.

> The 'psychological' and the 'physical' are indifferent to the real process. The 'functional' significance for the whole is alone relevant. Although we are forced to employ these descriptive terms, in other words, to speak of physical and psychological phenomena, we must always bear in mind that, in doing so, we are dealing with data which have to be evaluated in the light of their functional significance of the whole.
>
> We are always dealing with the activity of the whole organism, the effects of which we refer at one time to something called mind, at another time to something we call body. In noting an activity, we describe the behaviour of the whole organism either through the index of the so-called mind or through the index of the body.

2. The verbal expression of Alexander's head, neck and back pattern is 'neck free, head forward and up, back lengthening and widening'.

It may be desirable to give additional clarification to the term 'head forward and up'.

The anatomical equivalent of the term 'head forward' depends on how the head is placed at the beginning. The motion is a rotation in the median plane which brings the eye-ear plane approximately parallel to the ground.

The phrase 'head up' means head vertically upward in relation to the ground. Anatomically, one would say in a superior direction.

A detailed and explicit account of Alexander's HN & B pattern is given in Chapter 13, page 134.

B. Comments of John Dewey, Sir Charles Sherrington and G. E. Coghill on Alexander's search and discovery

Comments of John Dewey, philosopher and educator, in his Introduction to Alexander's book, *The Use of the Self.**

They [all interested people] will find a record of long continued, patient, unwearied experimentation and observation on which every inference is extended, tested, corrected by further more searching experiments; they will find a series of such observations in which the mind is carried from observation of comparatively coarse, gross, and superficial connections of causes and effect to those causal conditions which are fundamental and central in the use which we make of ourselves.

Personally, I cannot speak with too much admiration—in the original sense of wonder as well as the sense of respect—of the persistence and thoroughness with which these extremely difficult observations and experiments were carried out. In consequence, Mr Alexander created what may truly be called a physiology of the living organism. His observations and experiments have to do with the actual functioning of the body, with the organism in operation, and in operation under the ordinary conditions of living—rising, sitting, walking, standing, using arms, hands, voice, tools, instruments of all kinds. . . .

The vitality of a scientific discovery is revealed and tested in its power to project and direct new further operations which not only harmonize with prior results but which lead on to new observed materials, suggesting in turn further experimentally controlled acts, and so on in a continued series of new developments. Speaking as a pupil, it was because of this fact as demonstrated in personal experience that I first became convinced of the scientific quality of Mr Alexander's work. Each lesson was a laboratory experimental demonstration. Statements made in advance of consequences to follow and the means by which they would

---

* Reproduced by kind permission of E. P. Dutton, New York, and Methuen, London.

be reached were met with implicit scepticism—a fact which is practically inevitable, since, as Mr Alexander points out, one uses the very conditions that need re-education as one's standard of judgement. Each lesson carries the process somewhat further and confirms in the most intimate and convincing fashion the claims that are made.

From one standpoint, I had an unusual opportunity for making an intellectual study of the technique and its results. I was, from the practical standpoint, an inept, awkward and slow pupil. There were no speedy and seemingly miraculous changes to evoke gratitude emotionally, while they misled me intellectually. I was forced to observe carefully at every step of the process and to interest myself in the theory of the operations. I did this partly from my previous interest in psychology and philosophy and partly as a compensation of my practical backwardness. In bringing to bear whatever knowledge I already possessed—or thought I did—and whatever powers of discipline in mental application I had acquired in the pursuit of these studies, I had the most humiliating experience of my life, intellectually speaking. For to find that one is unable to execute directions, including inhibitory ones, in doing such a seemingly simple act as sitting down, when one is using all the mental capacity which one prides himself of possessing, is not an experience congenial to one's vanity.

. . . In re-affirming my conviction as to the scientific character of Mr Alexander's discoveries and technique, I do so then not as one who has experienced a 'cure', but as one who has brought whatever intellectual capacity he has to the study of a problem.

The following quotation is from the book of the physiologist Sir Charles Sherrington, *The Endeavour of Jean Fernel*.*

> Mr Alexander has done a service to the subject [will and reflex action] by insistently treating each act as involving the whole integrated individual, the whole psychophysical man. To take a step is an affair not of this or that limb solely but of the total neuromuscular activity of the moment—not least of the head and neck.

---

* University Press, Cambridge.

The following quotations are from the 'Appreciation' written by the biologist G. E. Coghill at the beginning to Alexander's book, *The Universal Constant in Living.**

> The practice of Mr F. Matthias Alexander in treating the human body is founded, as I understand it, on three well-established biological principles:
>
> 1) that of the integration of the whole organism in the performance of particular functions,
> 2) that of proprioceptive sensitivity as a factor in determining posture,
> 3) that of the primary importance of posture in determining muscular action.
>
> These principles I have established through forty years of anatomical and physiological study of amblystoma of embryonic and larval stages and they appear to hold for other vertebrates as well. . . . He has further demonstrated the very important psychological principle that the proprioceptive system can be brought under conscious control and can be educated to carry to the motor centres the stimulus which is responsible for the muscular activity which brings about the manner of working [use] of the mechanism of correct posture. . . . In the development of Amblystoma— an appropriate posture is assumed at intervals an appreciable time before the particular muscular pattern is geared into action. This occurs in the development of swimming or walking and of feeding. Posture, therefore, is a fore-runner of action and must be regarded as basic to it.
> . . . These are the simple rudiments of movement which Mr Alexander calls into play by his methods of re-education. For he is pre-eminently an educator. He seeks to restore the functions of the body through their natural uses. This method of doing this is original and unique, based as they are on many years of experience and exhaustive study. Yet, they can scarcely be adequately described, although the results are marvellous. . . . He [Alexander] enabled me to prevent misdirection of the muscles of my neck and back and to bring about use of these muscles that determine the

---

* Reproduced by kind permission of E. P. Dutton, New York.

relative position of my head and neck to my body and so on to my limbs, bringing my thighs into the abducted position. [Coghill has complained in a previous paragraph that the habitual use of the chair tends to produce adduction of the thighs.] This led to changes in the muscular and other conditions throughout my body and limbs associated with a pattern of behaviour more natural (in agreement with the total pattern) for the act of getting on my feet (from a chair); the whole procedure was calculated to occupying my brain with the projection of directive messages that would enable me to acquire conscious control of the proprioceptive component of the reflex mechanism involved. The projection of the directed messages, Mr Alexander considers, stimulated nervous and motor activity associated with better conditions. This leads to the belief that the *motor paths of the spinal cord and the nerve paths through the brain associated with the total pattern* were again being used.

It is my opinion that the habitual use of improper reflex mechanism in sitting, standing and walking introduces conflict in the nervous system and that conflict is the cause of fatigue and nervous strain which bring many ills in their train. Mr Alexander, by relieving this conflict between the total pattern which is hereditary and innate, and the reflex mechanisms which are individually cultivated, conserves the energies of the nervous system and by so doing corrects not only natural difficulties but also many other pathological conditions that are not ordinarily recognized as postural. This is a corrective principle that the individual learns for himself and is the work of the self as a whole. It is not a system of physical culture which involves only one system of organs for better or for worse of the economy of the whole organism. Mr Alexander's method lays hold of the individual as a whole, as a self-vitalizing agent. He reconditions and re-educates the reflex mechanisms and brings their habits into normal relation with the functions of organisms as a whole. I regard his methods as thoroughly scientific and educationally sound.

C. Review by Marjory Barlow of Lulie Westfeldt's *F. Matthias Alexander*

Reprinted from *The Alexander Journal*
no. 5, 1966, pp. 30–31

The chief value of this book lies in the account given by one of Alexander's first students of her experiences in learning and teaching the Technique. Miss Westfeldt writes with deep understanding of the principles underlying Alexander's discovery, and of the value of the application of these principles in restoring the normal working of 'the laws of the organism'. There is a great deal in the book which will enlighten and stimulate anyone who is using the Technique. It is a story of remarkable achievement and adventure in the new field of knowledge opened by Alexander.

The title of the book is in some ways misleading, containing as it does more autobiography than biography. We learn a great deal about Miss Westfeldt—her patient persistence and dedication to the work, and her delightful qualities of frankness and humour. Anyone who was in the first training course will appreciate her gift of evocation in the description of Ashley Place in those days.

The reader would do well, however, to remember the obvious truth that the same events and situations can be given different interpretations by different people. In many respects Miss Westfeldt's analysis of Alexander is perceptive and generous. The real stature of the man emerges clearly. An original thinker is certain to be to some extent 'a law unto himself', and Alexander was no exception. As Miss Westfeldt says, the very qualities which made his achievements possible were sometimes a cause of difficulty between him and his associates. To those who thought that he could do no wrong disillusionment was inevitable. The failure to see him as a human being as well as a great teacher, and inability to separate the man and his work, sometimes led to rejection of both. The best course was to seek to understand why his behaviour was sometimes so surprising. In order to clarify possible bafflement about the interpretation of Alexander's character given in this book some alternative suggestions will be put forward, not necessarily more valid and, no doubt, equally subjective.

I do not agree with the author on the reasons for Alexander's delay in starting a training course. In the best tradition of all great teachers, he preferred to teach the individual and to train people on the apprenticeship basis. This involved having one or two students at a time, who gained their understanding and practical experience by working closely with the teacher. The second reason, often expressed in my hearing, was that Alexander had had a very hard struggle in building his teaching practice. He did not feel justified in encouraging others to take up the profession until he felt some assurance that they would be able, when qualified, to earn a living. By 1931 the work was receiving so much support that he believed that the time had come to increase the number of teachers. In this decision he was taking upon himself the third big task that his work entailed. The first was the discovery of the Technique itself, the second task was learning to impart what he knew to others. This involved training his hands in the skill required. The third task was to learn how to teach others to teach, a very different matter. It must have seemed a formidable job to a man who preferred individual, or small group contact with others, to working with large numbers. Alexander was at his best, I think, with a group of three or four students; and the initial training course saw his first attempt at teaching a large group.

It was not my impression that he was bored by the training sessions—I think he was sometimes exasperated by us and disappointed by our inability to grasp what was to him so luminously clear and simple. With regard to Miss Westfeldt's analysis of his motives and conduct during the production of the Shakespeare plays, my impressions were different from hers. We had intensive training in using and projecting our voices and in the use of the jaw, lips, tongue, etc.—knowledge which is essential for work with pupils who have voice and speech difficulties due to misuse of these overworked parts. Also we learned a great deal by being forced to apply the work, not only in everyday life and in working on each other, but in a highly exacting art like stagecraft.

Alexander felt an enormous burden of responsibility for 'the work' as he always called it. He had a very objective view of it and of its importance which seemed to be quite apart from him personally. It was as if he saw himself as a necessary instrument in making it available but did not regard it as 'his'. One favourite remark was 'If I had not found it some other poor chap would have had to go through all that—the need for it was there.' Because of this he often appeared to guard it jealously—especially when 'opportunities' were offered which he thought might endanger the purity of the principles by which he worked. He was realistic enough to know that much remained to be discovered in extending the scope and application of the work. 'Remember that we are only on the fringe of this new knowledge,' he would say. He emphasized the need for a teacher to develop his own way of passing on the Technique. Very often he would warn us: 'Don't copy *me*. I don't want a lot of monkeys imitating me. Watch what I do and understand *why* I do it, then you will find your own method of achieving the result.' He knew that wide variation in teaching method was inevitable and desirable so long as the essence of his discoveries was not abandoned. He expected us to show initiative and make discoveries for ourselves and would not 'spoon-feed' us. As Miss Westfeldt says: 'He was a genius, going his own way with strength, impervious to the opinions of others, having different values as to what was important, attending to different things.'

In the technical parts of this book it is clearly brought out that the teacher's main responsibility is to make the pupil understand how to work on himself. It is important to remember that the only means that Alexander had at his disposal was the power to inhibit his immediate response to a stimulus and the ability to re-pattern the habitual misuse of his body by sending conscious directions to it. He did not have the help of a teacher's skilled hands to give him experience of the new use of himself. To quote him again: 'Anyone can do what I do *if* they will do what I did.' Miss Westfeldt demonstrates the truth of this statement and disproves his rider: 'But none of you want the discipline.'

D. Extract from a letter dated 20th November 1934 addressed to Irene Tasker

Hamlet was simply marvellous! I don't know if the theatre was full but it certainly seemed it.

F. M. made up very well indeed and looked quite young on the whole. Mummy was not sure which of the two performances she liked him in best, in *The Merchant of Venice* or *Hamlet* but I think that on the whole *Hamlet* gave him better chances and of course he was marvellous.

All the students were very improved and somehow much more finished than before. I thought Gurney was especially improved as the King. Goldie seemed *much* better than before: She appeared to have much more confidence and looked very nice in a white frock as Ophelia.

When she becomes mad she didn't overact but was horribly realistic and seemed to hold everyone's attention.

There was absolutely no stage scenery except what was necessary—nothing like as elaborate as the *Merchant*, and although F. M. was afraid that the students would find the large stage difficult, there was never any muddle and every detail appeared thought out.

I thought it was rather bad luck that they should have a bad start. The curtains drew back and the orchestra went on playing; it was very annoying as they did not realise for a few minutes that the play had started. F.M. had to be prompted twice and Marjory Mechin gave a goblet on the stage a kick and it rolled slowly across the stage and dropped into the footlights with a bang! A few people laughed but she was not a bit upset and went on quite calmly.

The play went much too quickly and the papers were quite nice in their criticisms. It was a jolly good show and we all enjoyed it.

A second letter

F. M. gave a very beautiful performance as Hamlet, very restrained and very fine, and his voice was splendid—one heard every word even when he seemed to be speaking softly. He is a marvel.

George Trevelyan was good in both his parts and looked very attractive as Laertes. Jean MacInnes was rather weak I thought—the least good anyway. Marjory managed Horatio wonderfully well and Erica was very good as the courtier. Miss Goldie was very good, especially in the mad scene... I would like to see John Gielgud now. It struck me that the description of his Hamlet rather tallied with Mr Alexander's. I should imagine they have taken the same view of the part and might play it in rather the same way.

E. Newspaper Reviews of 'Hamlet'

Alexander Trust Fund
Performance of 'Hamlet'

In aid of the F. Matthias Alexander Trust Fund, a performance of *Hamlet* was given at the Old Vic last night by Mr F. M. Alexander and the students of his training course.

The course teaches a technique of control in the everyday acts of life, and none of the students taking part in the performance could claim any theatrical experience. For them the play was an opportunity to control speech, movement, gesture and expression in the light of the general instruction received in the training course. They mostly acquitted themselves well in the difficult and unfamiliar conditions of the tragic stage. Mr Alexander himself played Hamlet, allowing himself few gestures and hardly any show of passion, but achieving what effects lie within the compass of a trained reciter. Mr George Trevelyan, in the part of Laertes, proved himself a sound elocutionist, and Miss Margaret Goldie spoke Ophelia's lines with rhythm and clearness, and showed a sense of the stage. Miss Marjory Mechin had the distinction of playing Horatio and she deserved it.

The Times, 14 November 1934

Training School Actors' 'Hamlet'
– New Methods Displayed

The production of *Hamlet* staged at the Old Vic last night by F. Matthias Alexander and his pupils was in one way unique. With the possible exception of Mr Alexander himself, not one of the cast had any real acting experience, even as an amateur; and in spite of that the performance was a good one.

Mr Alexander is the inventor of a system for teaching self-knowledge and self-control, and the head of a training school. It certainly speaks well for his methods that his pupils were able to bear themselves with such confidence and to speak so clearly that their manifest lack of stage technique was discounted. Mr George Trevelyan, as Player King, spoke his lines particularly well.

In the part of Hamlet Mr Alexander had obviously an advantage over his company. Thirty years ago, before he became a teacher, he was an elocutionist; and the fact was apparent last night. There was balance, rhythm, and intelligence in every line that he spoke.

The Daily Telegraph, 14 November 1934

/ conscious control /
no - psycho-physical
use + function
habit

INDEX

Alexander, Albert R. 27, 32, 34, 45, 48, 95, 99–100; *fig.* 4 40
Alexander, Edith Mary 46; *fig.* 5 47
Alexander, F. M.: in USA 11, 95; first meeting with Westfeldt 19–24; fees 24; hands 25; use of words 28, 50; teaching on training course 35; on mental order 36; proposed foundation 39; in company 39, 42; opportunities 39, 67; reciting 41; riding 43; interests 44; betting 44, 45; being bored 45–46; family life 46–48 *passim*, 95; Ludovici's book 53; proposed school 66; proposed teachers society 67, 97; on Jesus Christ 69; acting 72–73; strength 76; in Hamlet 79, 171, 172, 173; on Westfeldt 95; discovery of HN & B pattern 125–127, 129–131; as genius 127; life in Tasmania 128–129; and anatomists 159; *fig.* 1 20; *fig.* 3 38; *fig.* 4 40; *fig.* 5 47
Alexander, Max: *fig.* 2 33
Alexander, Peggy 46, 47, 48, 95
Alexander Teachers Society 67, 97
Alexander Trust Fund, The 51, 71, 172
American foundation for the work 39
Anatomy and the Problems of Behaviour (G. E. Coghill) 58
angina pectoris 108
ankle 4, 5, 6, 13, 22, 87, 89, 102, 103
arms: *fig.* 19 140
Asche, Oscar xii
Ashley Place 24, 27, 43, 45, 48, 59, 61, 72, 93, 94, 95, 168; 'Blues' 73; *fig.* 2 33; teaching room 23–24
Atlantic Monthly, The 11

attitudinal reflexes 70

Bach, Reginald 73, 74, 79
Barlow, Dr Wilfred 61, 110, 121
Barlow, Marjory 33, 168, 171, 172
Barstow, Majorie: *fig.* 2 33
Beerbohm, Lady 20
belief 68, 69
Billiard Marker, The 41
Brayton, Lily xii
Brooks, Sarah 40
Brown, Mrs 11, 20, 24, 59, 99

Cafe Royal 45
calf muscles 29
case history: angina pectoris (S. B.) 108; athlete (J. B.) 120–121; badminton (B. D.) 116–117; blood circulation (G.D.) 109; childhood polio 108; D. M. 112; eyestrain (E. B.) 107; numb leg (R. D.) 117–120; pain (M. F.) 114–116; riding accident (B.J.) 112–114; trouble with foot (L. C.) 108; woman with polio 108
Central Control 69, 70
civilization 148
Clayden, Mr Justice 96
Coghill, George E. xii, 58, 129, 131, 150, 166
Collier, Constance xii
Conference of the Associations of Commerce of the 91
Constructive Conscious Control of the Individual (F. M. Alexander) 152 Conscious Control 47
Cripps, Lady Isobel xii, 97
Cripps, Sir Stafford xii, 27, 67, 97

Daily Telegraph, The 79
'*der Tag*' 37, 53, 67
Derby 39, 44
Dewey, John xii, xvi, 20, 96, 135; on Alexander's search 164; on

Index

inhibition 152
direct, direction 25, 50, 51, 134, 164. *See also* order, ordering
Donat, Robert 41
'dowager's hump' 61
Duke, J. B. 21

Egyptian figure: *fig.* 16 136
end-gaining 117
Endeavour of Jean Fernel, The (Charles Sherrington) 165
Ends and Means (Aldous Huxley) 117, 160
Etruscan Warrior *fig.* 21 143
eyes, improvements in 107

feelings 64, 101, 113, 146–148, 147, 149, 151; unreliable 27, 146
foot, feet 4, 5, 7, 8, 13, 22, 57, 59, 87, 88, 89, 103, 108, 109, 111; flat 12
Frank, Alma 150

Gobbo, Launcelot 74–76, 79
Goldie, Margaret 171, 172; *fig.* 2 33
Goldstein, Kurt 163
Goodlief, Leonard 45
'grasshopper' suit 44

Hamlet 76, 80, 171; Programme, *fig.* 9 74; *fig.* 10 75
hands: position of 30
head forward 50, 51, 64, 81, 82, 102, 131, 137, 138, 139, 144, 163; and down 52; *fig.* 18 139; confusion about 137; discussion of 137; *fig.* 17 138; *fig.* 17, 18 138
head forward and up 18, 35, 102, 107, 113, 134, 137, 144, 163
Health and Education Through Self-Mastery (A. Ludovici) 52
heel 6, 87, 90, 91, 102, 103
hero-image 49, 53
HN & B pattern: description 134–144; introduction 18
Hughes, George 137
Huxley, Aldous xii, 93, 117, 118, 156, 157, 159

infantile paralysis 16, 30, 107. *See also* polio
inhibition 18, 25, 26, 35, 103, 104, 107, 117, 152, 152–153, 154, 155, 160; introduction 19; John Dewey on 152
Irving, Sir Henry xii, 20, 40

Jacks, L. P. 52, 53, 76
James, William 129
jaw 50, 58, 81, 169
Jokl, Dr Ernst 96
Jones, Dr Ernest 127

knee 27, 90, 91, 102, 110, 112, 113, 117; in monkey 35; thrust 41
knee thrust: *fig.* 21 143

Lang, Matheson xii, 20, 40
Lawrence, Esther 38, 65, 66, 67, 80, 82
Libel Action (Alexander *vs.* Jokl) 96
Little School 43, 59, 61, 65
Ludovici, Anthony 38, 52, 53, 76
lumbar spine 19
Lytton, Lord xii, 21

Macdonald, Patrick 33
MacInnes, Gurney 171; *fig.* 2 33; *fig.* 4 40; *fig.* 11 78; *fig.* 12 78
MacInnes, Jean 172; *fig.* 2 33
MacLeish Archibald 101
Magnus, Rudolf 69, 70, 129, 131
Man's Supreme Inheritance (F. M. Alexander) 3, 134
Merchant of Venice, The 46, 66, 71, 79, 82, 83, 171; Programme, *fig.* 8 72
Mikado, The 41
monkey position 35

Napoleon 42
National Gallery 29
neck forward: and down: *fig.* 22 145
neck free 18, 101, 113, 135, 137, 139, 144, 163
Neil, Charles 33; *fig.* 11 78
nervous tension 12
Nora (pupil of Westfeldt) 104, 106; drawing of cat, *fig.* 15 106

Old Vic 71, 79
order, ordering 25, 35, 51, 115, 134, 135. *See also* direct, direction
Organism, The (Kurt Goldstein) 163

pattern 19, 22, 120, 121. *See also* HN & B pattern; body 26, 58, 109, 153; connecting 132; dynamic 132; faulty 26; habit 120; main 58, 84; motion 113; muscular 26, 105, 166; neuromuscular 106, 155; new 115, 132, 146, 147, 152, 154; of back 30; old 19, 26, 105, 152, 153; partial 58, 59, 84; total 22, 58, 59, 167; wrong 106
pelvis 18, 91, 99, 136, 140, 149
Penhill 41, 43, 44, 45, 46, 61, 69
Philosopher's Stone, The (J. H. Robinson) 11
Pilgrim's Progress (Bunyan) 86
Poetry and Experience (Archibald MacLeish) 101
polio xiii, 4, 6, 7, 8, 9, 22, 23, 102, 107, 108. *See also* infantile paralysis
primary control 10, 12, 22, 23, 69, 70, 83

Race, The 41
rib cage 19, 142, 143
Robinson, James Harvey xii, 11, 21
Rose (gardener) 43
Rowntree, Joseph 136

Sadler's Wells 71, 80
saliva 108
Sandow, Eugene 21
Saturday Review of Literature 156
Saturday Review, The 127
school for children, proposed 65
sciatica 110
Selye, Dr Hans 128
sensory: re-education 147; registration 64
Shakespeare, William 41
Shaw, Bernard xii
Sherrington, Sir Charles 165
shoulder-blades 8, 86, 142, 143, 150
Shylock 72
Silcox, Lucy 15, 16, 17, 20

skin, improvements in 107
Smith, Dr Millard 149
Smuts, General 92
sore spots, disappearance of 109
Spencer, Herbert 57
Spicer, Dr Robert 39
St Felix's School 15
Stewart, Irene: *fig.* 2 33; *fig.* 11 78
students: improvements 61–62
Student's Room 36
'Study in Infant Development, A' (Alma Frank) 150; *fig.* 23 151
suit of armour: *fig.* 19 140; *fig.* 20 141
Susan (pupil of Westfeldt) 102–103

Tasker, Irene 171
Tattenham Corner 39
Temple, William xii, 21
Times, The xii
Tomorrow and Tomorrow and Tomorrow (Aldous Huxley) 157
training course: reappraisal 54
tranquillity 110
Tree, Viola xii, 20, 40
Trevelyan, George 172, 173; *fig.* 12 78; *fig.* 2 33; *fig.* 4 40
'turn' 49

Universal Constant in Living, The (F. M. Alexander) 95, 117, 150, 166
Use of the Self, The (F. M. Alexander) 69, 146, 164

walking: *fig.* 20 141
Webb, Ethel 24, 25; *fig.* 4 40
Welch, Jimmy 40
Westfeldt, Lulie: *fig.* 2 33; *fig.* 4 40; *fig.* 6 60
When Knights Were Bold 40
Whittaker, Erika 172; *fig.* 2 33; *fig.* 4 40
Wielopolska, Catherine 3, 9, 10, 11, 12, 14, 20, 33; *fig.* 4 40
Winged Victory (Nike) of Samothrace 61; *fig.* 7 63
Wood, Eleanor (daughter) 15
Wood, Mrs 15, 19
writing 104–105, 106

York, the Duke of 92